ONE MORE LIGHT

ONE MORE LIGHT

*Life, Death and Humanity
Through a Firefighter's Eyes*

JAMES GEERING

BEHIND THE SHIELD LLC

This hardback edition published 2022 in the United States of America by Behind the Shield LLC

www.jamesgeering.com

ISBN 978-1-7355868-2-3

Copyright © 2022 James Geering

Previous formats published 2020

ISBN 978-1-7355868-0-9 (paperback)
ISBN 978-1-7355868-1-6 (ebook)

The author asserts his moral right to be identified as the author of this book.

All rights reserved. No part of this publication may be reproduced, stored in a retrieval system, distributed or transmitted, in any form or by any means, without the prior permission in writing of the publisher or as expressly permitted by law.

Cover design by Margarita Felix, 100 Covers
Author photograph on cover by Dan Faenza
Interior design and layout by Daisy Editorial

Dedication

THIS BOOK IS DEDICATED to everyone on planet earth who has lost someone way too soon. I hope this honours their memory in some small way.

Foreword

BY JOSH BROLIN

I MET JAMES GEERING through our mutual friend Amanda Marsh. She is the widow of Eric Marsh, one of the 19 Granite Mountain firefighters who died in the Yarnell Fire on June 28th, 2013. He reached out to me through her to be a guest on his podcast Behind the Shield. We ended up having a nice conversation, an easy one. I liked what questions he asked. They weren't typical celebrity questions. He cared more about talking about firefighters and what was going on in the world, and he intrinsically picked up that I did too. An immediate friendship was forged.

Then the Malibu fires hit. We talked more, and the more we spoke the more I enjoyed and appreciated his perspective. I would call randomly, just to toss conversation around, knowing I would end up better off than when it started. We would talk about kids, leadership, mental health, community, frustrations, joys, and we'd always end with a few horror stories, just to keep it grounded and humbled. It was very apparent to me that these were two guys who wanted the best for themselves in the most big-picture context. I found someone who cared as much as I had just as I was getting more frustrated with what I felt was a progressively callused and more self-serving world. I felt myself contracting. The timing was moving. I always see these things as a little more than human, a little closer to something like little spiritual wake-ups when your life gets suddenly enhanced by someone else for reasons you won't understand until later. He's been that for me.

So right now, I am up on our family's ranch alone. It is quiet. I've been asked by James to write a foreword for the book he has now completed. The book whose chapters he has sent to me again and again to read and reread. The book that has made me cry several times over. This book.

I have come up here to write. The stars are incredibly bright tonight and the bend in the sky, the dome, is visible: you lie down, turn your head to the right and you are still looking up at the stars. The frogs are huffing, and you can hear the soft landing of each deer hoof as it tries to pass unnoticed in the dark. I've been out here for twenty minutes. I paused what I was watching inside: a behind the scenes of *Raging Bull*. As I lie here remembering why I love this area so much, this solitude, I am thinking about the film and how all those involved, during their respective interviews, were talking about behavior: that fascination of what makes us do what we do and why. Then I look at the sky and I'm humbled by the fact that it's obvious that we sometimes forget to feel, to notice, to take in the necessary subtleties. We forget to say hello and take a moment to tell someone we are thinking about them. We decide not to write a letter, or not to personalize a gift and to order it on Amazon instead, the gift card arriving blank.

We decide to be accepting of those who are suffering from abuse, obesity, PTSD, mental illness because with action we might be shamed, and with that in the air we choose to look away. We categorize by political party, race, wealth or lack thereof: the West, the South, the North, East Coast, "foreigners". We run run run and we resort to heroes: those with conviction, anyone not willing to back down, somebody "patriotic", almost pathologically unwavering. We forget what personal is, as we get mired in the definition of things and we spend most of our time making sure that our karate stance is better than the bad guy's. And the more time that goes by, the more we perceive others to be bad.

And then your daughter dies. Or your mother. Or your best friend. You remember, specifically, what their skin felt like the last time you grazed it as they walked by. You remember them smelling their favorite flower at some point during a walk you took with them. You are raw and in that rawness you have only one feeling and it is loss. And with loss comes humility. And with humility comes compassion. And with compassion comes a deep need for love: to give it, and to receive it.

You catch yourself thinking that you would just like to see them one last time. Say a few last words. Hug them.

We have to survive horrible moments but people, ultimately, are our nourishment, and care is our warriorship.

James Geering wrote a book that took my breath away with the level of compassion and care that it holds. Every chapter deals with a different trajectory of experience and issue, yet the through line of these more than rich chapters is that life is random (even with God at hand) and that without us sacrificing a few selfish comforts and focusing a little more on a deeper respect for our lives and the lives of others, the play in it, the gift of it, we are indeed dying one day at a time, instead of living one day at a time.

There are a few people in everyone's life who stand out. You remember them at the strangest of times. They are conjured when you need a voice that pushes you forward, when bravery is in question, when integrity for a moment floats in the ether.

It could be a schoolteacher you had as a child, maybe how your mother held you after she thought you had disappeared forever, or it may be the voice of your children, a grandmother, something you once read. People. They all come from people.

And so James Geering, in his quest to remind us that we are interested in being our best selves, illustrates his experiences of our best and our worst. He also reminds us that greed can get in the way of our wellbeing and that The Man may not always be looking out for our best interests. He reminds us that it takes energy to not only care but to take action on that compassion. Ultimately, he reminds us that the superhero has the potential to exist in us all, by showing up and taking responsibility when life's randomness rears its ugliest head and we are put to the test.

My wife, for my 52nd birthday, had a small writer's hut built for me. It is based on Dylan Thomas's boat house in South Wales; Laugharne, in fact. She had it built while I was gone, and so I came home to a raw version of my childhood dream come true. Unpainted. I went to the paint store, found that powder Irish green that had always inspired me so, and went on to, with one brush, paint furiously over a three-day period.

Every time I walk into that hut, it is mine. My paint. My tacked-up inspiration photos. My books on the makeshift shelf above. My small chosen desk against the windows that we purchased in a flea market for almost nothing in downtown Los Angeles. My reading chair.

I mention it as there is a lot to be said for ownership, the personalizing of your time here. Every decision is that: a draftsman's drawing of the foundation of your character. And at the end, whenever that end may come, that's what we will be confronted with – the house we built for ourselves. How did we affect those around us? What did we stand for? How willing were we to take a step toward the deep footprint our hearts can make in someone else's. Or did we contract, and shy away from what could have been the richest part of us realized?

We walk the razor's edge between communal worth and social numbing, essentially, and what we lean more toward will determine the memory of us as a collective. For our children. For theirs.

James Geering is a great friend, and a mentor, of sorts. I am inspired by his candor, and I am moved by his bravery. I've always loved firefighters. One of my best, lifelong friends is a firefighter in Tucson, Arizona: Fireman Dan, my kids know him as. Danny Martin. And, like James, he is experienced in pain. He's seen it all. And from that comes a toughness, but from that also comes a deep sensitivity towards humanity.

I look up to anyone who's been there, and has the courage to look behind the cosmetics of our corporate mentality. Big tobacco sat in front of the highest court and blatantly said that cigarettes are not addictive. Well, they are, and they still kill a lot of people. It an undeniable fact.

So James Geering took action, the same action he took as a firefighter. It's the same care he focused toward every person he put his boots on and answered the station bell for.

This book is a fire alarm wake-up call from a person who has been there.

I hope you are as moved and motivated as I was reading it.

Sincerely and with much respect,

JOSH BROLIN

Author's Note

THIS BOOK WAS BORN out of tragedy. About ten years into my career as a firefighter/paramedic I attended the funerals of six firefighters. The causes of their deaths were a host of both physical and mental disease. That was also ten years of witnessing suffering and loss on the calls I ran in my career. As an exercise physiology graduate and lifelong athlete, I knew that there were answers to so many of the elements that steal our loved ones from us.

One sleepless night, I couldn't get the thoughts out of my mind so I sat down in a fire station office and wrote my very first blog post entitled "I wish my head could forget what my eyes have seen". A week later, it had gone viral. This made me realise that there was a hunger for physical and mental health solutions. The Behind the Shield Podcast became that solution as I brought experts in from all walks of life to discuss their work.

After almost four years of interviewing the greatest minds in wellness, the book was born. I am by no means masquerading as an expert; in fact, quite the opposite. This is a journey of an ordinary firefighter and student of wellness who got to peer behind the proverbial curtain to see what truly saves lives. I have interviewed some amazing guests who were at some of the most notorious and horrendous events in our history. That being said, that is a fraction of the population and this book aims to detail what every first responder sees.

These stories are all based on real events in my career but some names and details have been fictionalised to protect the identities of those involved. The goal of this book is to reduce pain and suffering, so I would not want a loved one to relive one of the tragedies their family member endured. These events were heartbreaking to witness and hard to relive, but they are invaluable in telling these much-needed stories.

Prologue

I WAS ONLY FOUR years old the day we almost died. *Tom and Jerry* was on the television as we sipped orange juice and ate chocolate biscuits in my grandparents' sitting room. Gappa, my grandfather, had caved in to our pleas to postpone lunchtime so we could find out how the little cartoon mouse would teach the grey cat a lesson. He had told us that we could finish the episode but had to eat right after. Gappa disappeared into the kitchen for a moment then walked back through the house. "Twenty minutes, no longer," he said in passing, the facade of sternness betrayed by the cheeky twinkle he always had in his eyes when joking with us.

Unbeknown to us, he had mistakenly turned the heat under the chip fat up instead of down before going into his study to play the piano.

Gappa was a skilled pianist and as a child I would sit for hours, perched next to him on the stool, as he played his favourite pieces. The bench was hollow, the padded top hinged open, revealing reams of classical music from Chopin to Mozart. A mahogany metronome would click and clack as his fingers danced across the keys, defying the arthritis that plagued them. His precision and grace told of decades of practice and passion. Immaculately dressed, he was never without a crisp pressed shirt, tie and silver cufflinks, hair always slicked back with Brylcreem. His head would tilt up and down, eyes darting from the page to his hands and back again.

As I sat there with my eight-year-old sister, Anna, and two-year-old brother, Tim, completely engrossed in the cartoon, we heard a loud pop. The glass panels of the dining room door were blackened. Anna opened the door and screamed as thick smoke poured in. The formal dining room, usually staged as if for some fancy wedding, was dark, the immaculate white place settings now cloaked in black soot. The taper candles had melted, pouring off the silver candelabras like a Salvador Dali painting. Flames licked from the kitchen beyond, growing with each breath of oxygen now introduced from the open door.

Our screams seemed like distant cries as my young mind tried to make sense of the chaos that unfolded before us. Anna started calling Gappa's name, unsure where he had gone. She ran to the front door and pulled, shrieking as the latch would not open. I'm not sure how my eight-year-old sister stayed so composed. She ran to the guest room upstairs and managed to call home. This was long before modern cell phones, compact, mobile and never far from the owner. Our old rotary phone must have rung in the kitchen repeatedly, echoing in the deserted farmhouse, far from the earshot of my mother. The flames from the rooms below licked at the upstairs window, sending my sister running back downstairs.

Anna raced back to the front door, pulling as hard as she could, adrenaline now fuelling her actions. By this time, the living room was rapidly filling with smoke, displacing the oxygen with a cocktail of poisonous gases from the burning furniture. I still remember the front door flying open as she yanked with all of her might. I grabbed Tim's hand and we ran out into the garden, collapsing on the soft green grass. We lay there, taking deep breaths of the cool spring air and coughing out the noxious fumes that filled our lungs. I don't remember any of us crying; we just lay there, stunned by the life-changing shift from watching cartoons to a near-death experience.

Amid the crackling of the fire, a gut-wrenching howl filled the air. Gang Gang and Gappa's dog Holly was trapped on the other side of the house. We ran over to the utility room door. A silhouette of the poodle frantically scratched at the frosted glass, crying in fear and pain. Anna found a stick and tried to shatter the pane. She hit it repeatedly, but it was designed to withstand damage from the elements and refused to be breached. She smashed a window close to the door, trying to rescue their beloved pet, but it was too little, too late. Holly's yelping stopped as the flames overcame her, a sound that haunts my sister to this day.

As we stood there, reeling from trauma, frantic voices began to permeate our consciousness. My grandparents' elderly neighbours stood at the wall separating the two properties. We ran to them and, one by one, we were lifted over to the safety of their garden. I looked back at the house, leaning on the rough grey brick, suddenly a distant observer of the tragedy we had just experienced. The downstairs fire had extended into the second floor, flames raging from the bedrooms above the kitchen, where Anna had been standing only moments earlier.

Upon seeing the fire, the neighbours had called 999. Sirens began to wail, growing louder as we were taken to another neighbour we knew two doors up the street. As the firefighters arrived, they found Gappa pulling weeds in the garden. The fire had sent him into such a deep shock that he had reverted to tending to the garden that he loved so much. In World War II, he had operated one of the anti-aircraft guns on the Orkney Islands, on the northernmost Scottish coast. His crew was credited with shooting down the first enemy bomber over Britain. Gappa never spoke of the war despite my childlike curiosity for all things military. It was as if he'd locked it away deep inside, far away from his outward-facing post-war role of pension advisor.

I wonder whether a lifetime of suppressing the horrors he saw finally took their toll as he knelt in that garden. Did the rolling clouds of smoke take him back to some macabre scene he witnessed protecting Scotland's shores?

Back at our farm, my mum had just got back from the stables when she heard the phone ringing.

"Hello, Mrs Geering?"

"Yes, who is this?"

"This is the emergency operator. There has been a fire at your father's house. I want to assure you that he is fine."

"Oh no! What about my children?" My mum was frantic.

There was a long pause. "Children?"

I can only imagine the dread that filled my mother at that moment. "My three children were staying with him. They were in the house. Are they alright?" Mum asked as a maelstrom of emotions flooded her.

"I … I'm not sure, Mrs Geering. I'll have to contact the fireground to find out."

"I'm coming now!" she shouted and hung up the phone.

My mother drove for twenty minutes, tears streaming down her face, sobbing uncontrollably. Each minute must have seemed like an hour, each mile like a hundred.

Back at the house, the fire was still being knocked down as the news was relayed that there were three kids missing. The scene rapidly shifted from an exterior operation to an aggressive interior search. Men who had been knocking down the blaze from the outside were now gearing up to go inside. One minute they were flowing water from a ground monitor in the garden, the next they were looking for the charred remains of three children. They searched everywhere they could, fire still raging on the second floor and in the roof. Every closet, bathtub and bed were frantically searched for some miracle, on the off chance that a child may have found refuge from the inferno they had witnessed.

Word finally reached the fireground that we were safely in the neighbour's home. I can only imagine the relief that must have swept over the entire scene.

I can still remember the moment my mother arrived, tears streaming down her face as she burst into the neighbour's living room. She hugged me so tightly, tears soaking my hair as she kissed the top of my head. There's a deep feeling of security being a child in your mother's arms. A sense that everything is okay now, no matter what you've just gone through. Trauma is a strange thing. It haunts some, a recurring nightmare they relive time and again. For me, this memory became locked away, deep in my mind. I'm not sure if it's because I was too young to process it or that I was more of a bystander while Anna took charge. I literally owe her my life. And that was the beginning of my journey to doing something with it.

Chapter One

I wish my head could forget what my eyes have seen.
– Dave Parnell

"I need help on the Charlie side!" The voice came over the radio as we sped towards the confirmed structure fire. The warm Florida air was tinged with the distinct smell of fire as it blew into the cab from the darkness beyond. Not just any fire, but the heartbreaking odour of someone's entire life going up in smoke. Neon signs blurred into streaks as Emma sped down the near-empty streets, siren wailing, the hustle and bustle of the daytime commuters replaced by the dubious activities of those who preferred doing business in the shadows. Men and women who hid from the police yet still waved to us as they probably had during childhood.

John, the medic on the radio, usually calm and collected, had an edge in his voice that I hadn't heard before. He was a salty little bugger but usually even-keeled under pressure. Fortunately, we hadn't quite reached the destination, so we were able to make a last-minute detour to his location, one street south of the dispatch address. As Emma made the turn, the street was illuminated by the orange glow of a fully involved single-storey house, flecked with the red and blue lights of the first responder vehicles in the neighbouring street. We pulled into a vacant space directly behind the engulfed home, heat palpable through the windshield despite the considerable distance.

Three people were at the edge of the garden, silhouetted by the inferno behind them. John and his partner were standing on one side of a four-foot chainlink fence. A hunched figure stood on the other side, smoke drifting lazily off his body. "Grab a backboard!" John shouted as I stepped out.

I ran to them while Emma grabbed the board from the compartment. The smouldering figure leant on the steel fence pole, head on his forearms. If he had been wearing clothes, they were long gone now.

John was clearly ruffled by what he had seen. "The neighbours said he ran out of the house on fire. They were putting him out with a garden hose when we got here."

As the man stood there, smouldering, Emma and I hopped over the fence and laid him down onto the backboard she had carried over. We had learned the manoeuvre in emergency medical services school: the standing takedown. Sitting in that classroom as an enthusiastic emergency services technician student in my pristine dark-blue uniform, I never envisioned using it this way. The injuries we saw while assessing him were what we call signs incompatible with life, yet this man was clearly far from dead. We buckled the straps and carefully lifted him over the fence onto the awaiting stretcher. At such times you are grateful for the physical training required of a firefighter. People are heavy and awkward, and the inability to rescue someone because of a lack of strength is not an option.

We pushed the stretcher through the soft, wet grass, mud clinging to the wheels, slowing our progress. The rear doors of the rescue vehicle were already open and we swiftly loaded the gurney into the patient compartment. The neon lights revealed the extent of the man's injuries with clinical clarity. Fire is unforgiving on human tissue. It had burned through his clothes, skin and fatty layers. His ears, nose and groin were reduced to ash, like a hearth after a winter log fire. Only the soles of his feet escaped the ferocity of the flames. They were pink and seemingly oblivious to the immense trauma the rest of his body had endured. The doors closed behind us and Emma began the short but speedy journey to the hospital.

As we repeated our assessment in the fluorescent light, the sense of helplessness was palpable. A paramedic can reverse a diabetic emergency with dextrose, counter an opioid overdose with Narcan or defibrillate a quivering heart back into a lifesaving rhythm. But burns leave a medic with only a handful of options. We can fight to prevent the airway from swelling closed, attempt to replace lost fluid, provide pain medication if the vital signs permit and try to protect compromised skin from infection. Outside of these procedures, the goal is simply to get the patient to a trauma centre as soon as possible. The skin is the body's primary defence system and once it has been compromised, an agonising journey of fasciotomies, debriding, grafts and powerful medications is the patient's only hope.

We began the lifesaving interventions even though we knew in the back of our minds that survival after these extreme burns was near impossible. As John continued his assessment and tried to cover the massive trauma, I set up to intubate. We hoped to place a tube that would stop the complete constriction of the patient's swelling airway, a literal race against time. As I leaned over him, surgical steel laryngoscope in one hand, tube in the other, John asked the patient his name, primarily to determine his level of consciousness. What happened next defies all anatomy and physiology.

With a nose reduced to ash, lips scorched, revealing a macabre skull-like smile, and a tongue shrivelled like a thirsty leech, he said his name was Jason. The speed and precision of his response defied everything I'd been taught in paramedic school. John looked at me incredulously, then asked him a follow-up question.

"How old are you, Jason?"

"Twenty-two," he replied.

His injuries meant there was no chance that any upper airway function was still intact yet his voice responded with uninjured clarity. The next question seemed obvious.

"Jason, on a scale of zero to ten, how would you rate your pain?"

"Zero," he replied. Every nerve ending in his body had been destroyed to the point where he was literally pain free.

This planet is inhabited by people with diverse spiritual, religious and philosophical beliefs, but what we saw could not be explained by science. Every anatomical element needed to create the spoken word had been destroyed. The voice we heard was that of a healthy, uninjured young man, a far cry from the scorched figure who lay in front of us. The disjointed spectacle jarred with the very core of my human experience. Never had I seen, nor would I witness again, a soul visibly separated from its mortal flesh.

As a medical professional, you want to take action that will improve the patient's condition. The fact that he was now talking to us derailed our options. Our protocols didn't allow for rapid sequence intubation, and we were literally five minutes from the trauma centre. He was pain free and we were unable to obtain vital signs because of the massive swelling all over his body. I grabbed an intraosseous drill and tried to find the landmark in his tibia through his swollen tissue. I thanked God it found its mark and sank the drill into the porous bone. I managed to squeeze some fluid into his rapidly depleting circulatory system, hoping to make some minute difference to the outcome.

As we pulled into the emergency room, the trauma staff were waiting by the door. John had called in a trauma alert so they knew we were bringing in a critical patient. As we wheeled Jason into the bay, the confusion of the doctors and nurses was obvious. Why was this severely burned patient wearing a non-rebreather mask? Where was the tube? Television makes ER transitions seem like a casual coffee shop conversation. The reality is that you have a host of medical professionals, each needing specific information to begin their roles in the patient's treatment. John began to recite the implausible story to the hospital team. Their initial cynicism was clear but then Jason spoke again. To their amazement, he continued to answer their questions as they performed well-rehearsed assessments and medical interventions. The initial looks of scepticism quickly turned to disbelief as they witnessed his words confound his anatomical trauma.

Another thing Hollywood gets wrong is that the paramedics get to follow the progress of the patient, hanging out for hours chatting to the beautiful doctors and nurses. The reality is that the next call is imminent and you are needed back in service as soon as possible. We walked out of the ER and stood there, shell-shocked, remembering our rescue. There is an eerie stillness looking into the empty box where moments ago you were fighting to save a life. The aftermath looks like a heartbreaking work of modern art. Medical equipment strewn on the bench, body fluids on the floor and discarded packets adorning every corner. The smell of burned flesh and clothes clinging to every surface, imprinting itself onto your olfactory system. We began the process of getting the rig ready for the next call. As we wiped down the equipment, restocked supplies and wrote up the report, disbelief still hung in the air.

Orlando had an insatiable appetite that night and, as soon as the truck was ready, we were off to the next call. Before long we were back at the hospital, the same one that would be flooded with dozens of shooting victims from the Pulse nightclub a few years later. As with most critical calls, I followed up on Jason. The ER staff told us that the young man we had rescued had passed away an hour after we left. Although we knew this was a foregone conclusion, you never get used to being unable to save a life.

This had been the deadliest day of my career. My shift had begun with a cardiac arrest. One of those terrible gastrointestinal bleeds that you know from the outset will not end well. The "codes" on television are clinically clean, with the patient waking up and hugging their rescuers two seconds after the body-jolting shock. What they don't show is the horrendous reality of fighting to save a body that has given up. Trying to secure an airway in a person who has a river of vomit pouring from their mouth. Suctioning the partially digested contents of their stomach, chunks of pizza overwhelming the narrow tubing. Trying to compress the chest of a quadriplegic whose ribs feel like the quarter panel of a car, rigid and immovable from decades of inactivity. I have been a firefighter for fourteen years and have never had a true "save" from a cardiac arrest. The constant inability to rescue the dying chips away at my psyche.

Around lunchtime that same day our neighbouring station responded to a car versus pedestrian incident. The driver had lost control and ploughed into a bus stop, trapping a woman under the sedan. The responding crews worked feverishly to free the woman from beneath the vehicle. Even drawing from the immense set of skills firefighters have to master, getting her out was complex. The car needed to be stabilised with telescoping jacks to control its movement. Airbags were then placed to slowly and deliberately lift the car enough to rescue the rapidly deteriorating woman. The firefighter role then switched to paramedic as wounds were dressed and tourniquets applied tightly to stem the life-threatening haemorrhage. Large-bore needles were placed and airway managed in the back of a speeding rescue vehicle, headed for the trauma centre where awaiting surgeons would fight to save her life.

Mid afternoon in the scorching August heat, we were toned out to a wellbeing check. A homeless woman had gone missing and we were called to help find her. We drove down Orange Avenue, one of Orange County's main artery roads, and tried to find a good access point to the woods she was known to inhabit. The area was a couple of densely wooded acres nestled in the heart of the Orlando urban sprawl. As we marched through the brush, it became evident that this poor woman had passed away. Decomposing flesh has an acrid, stomach-churning scent that affects the most primal senses in the body. As the lead medic, I went ahead alone, sparing the rest of my crew yet another macabre image in their mental filing cabinet of memories.

The woman's home was a collection of sheets and worn blue tarpaulins, hung from a frayed rope crudely strewn between oak trees. Old tyres were makeshift seats around a large wooden table made from a wire spool. Weathered aluminium pots and pans lay around a makeshift fire pit. Under one of the covers a dark figure lay on a stained mattress. The woman had been missing for three days and the Florida heat and animals had reduced her body to what looked like a charcoal caricature of a stick figure. Putrid flesh hung off bones, barely recognisable as a human being. It was a tragic realisation that a person could go unnoticed for three days in the middle of a bustling city. She was someone's daughter, maybe a mother, and yet she died alone surrounded by thousands of people. I said a silent prayer and returned to my crew and deputies to confirm our suspicions.

I tell these stories not to glorify the calls, although every good firefighter yearns to be there to help someone in their darkest hour. The point is to illustrate what people in our profession see throughout their career. Some days are uneventful, with the most memorable call involving strapping a rolled ankle or getting a child out of a locked car. On other days, however, things go bad. Really bad. Three years after this death-filled day, Orlando experienced the deadliest terror attack in the USA since 9/11. The Pulse nightclub, which was barely a mile from my area, was the scene of a homophobic-fuelled massacre that would test the mental and physical resilience of all who responded.

When we think of post-traumatic stress and the disorder PTSD, most people immediately think of our services personnel. Although the disorder is far from wholly accepted, the military forces have made huge leaps in addressing the effects of war on mental health. Sadly, it is still somewhat unacceptable for first responders to acknowledge this effect of their chosen profession. The facade of movie characters has distorted the image of what a "tough guy" should be. The vulnerability of real people has been replaced with John Wayne's Rooster or Sigourney Weaver's alien-slaying Ripley. The irony is that this couldn't be further from the truth, yet generations have clung to these fictional stereotypes. Those in crisis are met with responses like "Rub some dirt in it" or "Suck it up, buttercup".

The real men of Easy Company featured in the HBO classic *Band of Brothers* taught us a powerful lesson about the true cost of war. They spoke of the horrors that they had seen and done, still visibly crushed more than sixty years later. Their leader, Major Dick Winters, was moved to tears recalling the heroism of the men he served with. Likewise, a lifelong career as a firefighter, EMT or law enforcement officer is filled with the very worst life has to offer. I still see the faces of every bad call I've had, and at fourteen years my career is relatively short compared with many.

Trauma has badly affected people since the birth of humankind. It was mentioned in the *Epic of Gilgamesh*, which is considered to be the earliest surviving work of literature, with parts dating back to 2300BC. In the American Civil War, the effects of what we now call PTSD were referred to as "a soldier's heart". Some World War I veterans exhibited behaviour known as shell-shock. Battle fatigue was the label given to the World War II combatants with these symptoms. Many of the military members returning from Vietnam had what was described as "the thousand-yard stare". PTSD was finally acknowledged in the 1970s as scores of men and women returned from South East Asia a shadow of their former selves. Young Americans who had seen and done terrible things for their country were then thrust back into their communities without support.

Opinions of the war varied but there was a strong feeling of opposition. Unlike the returning heroes of World War II, there were no ticker tape parades welcoming the Vietnam veterans. These soldiers, sailors and airmen, who had been plucked from their communities to fight an unknown enemy, were shamed on their return. The trauma of combat was undoubtedly the primary cause of their mental anguish, but another element surfaced. While in combat, these men and women had been part of a cause, attached to a unit. During their time in the military, they were surrounded by their brothers and sisters, their tribe. For the duration of their active duty, they fought together, laughed together, ate and slept together. The removal from the unit was often more detrimental to the individuals than the horrors they had seen.

The advantage firefighters have is the brotherhood and sisterhood in the profession. Crews live together for hours to days at a time depending on the shift pattern. Some may even spend their entire career together. This cohesion provides a good outlet for the tragedy they encounter in the line of duty. For the outsider looking in, some may seem callous, making light of what they witness, but this support structure is invaluable, assuming there is a true closeness within that particular firehouse. The dinner table can be an incredibly powerful place to offload the trauma that we carry. Storytelling has been used in all human cultures to process war, loss and other challenges to the human psyche, and firefighters love to spin yarns.

When this support structure fails, those who had been relying on it find themselves without a foundation. Modern society is awash with electronic devices that connect us virtually yet disconnect us physically. By not engaging in true, honest conversations, we are losing the ability to offload and process the calls, family issues and other life stresses. Meaningful discussions over steaming mugs of coffee are being replaced by craned necks mindlessly scrolling through walls or feeds. Social media can be an incredibly positive tool, but more often than not it creates a rabbit hole of distraction, negativity and false narrative.

Another little-recognised factor that amplifies the mental health challenges is being removed from your "tribe". Whether the result of an injury, promotion to a desk job or simply retirement, being taken away from your crew can be incredibly detrimental if the effects are not recognised early. We have had a spate of suicides in the first responder community, and many of these men and women were either retired or at an officer level. There is no denying that losing the closeness of a band of brothers or sisters has a huge impact on your sense of belonging. To go from jumping on a rig with your crew and mitigating someone's worst day to shuffling papers in an office is a huge change for a career responder with lifesaving still burning in their heart.

A physical injury can be a double-edged sword. For a high-level tactical athlete to suddenly be incapacitated can be traumatic in itself. The more severe injuries can leave the responder questioning if they will ever be able to do the job they love again. The less acknowledged element of injury is its effect on mental health. To go from a busy firehouse to lying in a bed alone at home can be crushing. You don't know how healing a second family is until you are taken from it. This was to become all too apparent to me personally.

Another area rarely discussed is the mental effect of retirement. For many, the first responder profession is an honour, the badge on our chest representing an oath to protect our community. A career is full of both tragedy and joy. Some days you may make an incredible rescue, while on others you may watch someone die despite all of your valiant efforts. But one day will be your last. One day you'll step out of the fire station and the bay door will slowly close behind you. The stark realisation that the seat you occupied for decades will be immediately filled is like a punch to the gut.

That tight-knit crew you have seen and done so much with are now the other side of those doors. The mental showcase of tragedy is now yours to carry alone. For some, this change is smooth, with a host of new projects and social groups to smooth the transition. For others, however, the protector role may be an identity that they have clung to and have allowed to define them, and now it's being snatched away. The busy firehouse table may be replaced with a lonely apartment or empty home. The support structure that buffered a life of trauma is now greatly diminished.

This obviously parallels so many other professions, such as the military, nursing or a host of other careers that see things no one should ever have to. The anxiety and depression after a separation from the tribe make evolutionary sense too. Humans have been tribal for millennia, banding together for survival. If one member is separated, they are now vulnerable, so hypervigilance becomes a survival trait until they are reunited with their group. This is no different in modern society. There is a haunting irony that so many live in a city of millions and still feel deeply lonely. This concept is illustrated beautifully in Sebastian Junger's book *Tribe*, one that should sit on every human being's bookshelf.

As with many things in life, there is no one-size-fits-all solution to mental wellness. Each one of us has to navigate our own path to psychological and emotional health. Being aware of the contributing factors stacked against us is imperative. Once we can see the effects of childhood trauma, sleep deprivation, loss of tribe, guilt and shame, we can begin to create a roadmap back to our own version of harmony. The world is full of people with powerful stories overcoming immense tragedy to become an even more resilient version of themselves. We must learn from those who have walked through fire and made it out the other side.

Chapter Two

No man has the right to be an amateur in the matter of physical training. It is a shame for a man to grow old without seeing the beauty and strength of which his body is capable.

– Socrates

THE MORNING WAS SURPRISINGLY cool for South Florida as I stood in the shadow of a five-storey concrete drill tower that rose into the deep-blue sky. I was one of seventy candidates, all nervously anticipating the physical part of this multi-section testing process. The company had already delivered a written exam and an EMS skills test, sending our results to any fire department in their network that was hiring. My fellow candidates embodied a spectrum of shapes and sizes, ages and races. The feat ahead of us was basically an extension of the Firefighter Combat Challenge, performed wearing a brush jacket, helmet and gloves.

The test began with a five-storey stair climb carrying a relatively light highrise hose pack. Once at the top, a rolled hose was hoisted from the ground and pulled over the railing. The candidate then struck the Keiser sled from one end to the other before descending the tower. A moderate weight dummy was dragged a hundred feet and then a charged hose line was advanced. The test concluded when the last of three traffic cones was knocked down with the hose stream. For a well-prepared firefighter, this should have been tiring but very achievable in a good time.

As we nervously waited for our names to be called, I noticed two of the most orange human beings I've ever laid my eyes on. These gentlemen looked like they came from the womb of a promiscuous carrot. Based on the size of their muscles, I assumed that they'd had a little help from a pharmacist. The pair strutted around in t-shirts that must have been bought from Baby Gap, as though to intimidate the competition. Looking like the lovechild of Lou Ferrigno and a satsuma, they eyed the roost like farmhouse cockerels. As a rather scrawny academy graduate, I assumed that these two must be legends in the fire service, based on their confidence, self-love and sheer number of high fives.

What happened next was the beginning of a lifelong lesson on firefighter fitness. The first part of the physical test was climbing five floors with a hose pack. There were several candidates ahead of me so I had been watching to pick up any tips or tricks. As I looked up at the tower, an orange figure crawled up the third set of steel stairs in a state of complete exhaustion. Upon reaching the fourth floor, he dropped the hose and fell to the floor gasping for air. The moderator screamed at him, "Pick up the hose and keep climbing!" His words fell on deaf ears as the candidate visibly tapped out, ripping his helmet off dramatically. As if scripted, his pumpkin-spiced doppelganger stopped at the exact same place a minute later.

I don't mean to belittle them, but it was a huge illustration of how our perception of true fitness is very skewed. For decades we were taught that men should have giant chests and six-pack abs. "How much can you bench?" became the opening line in male conversations. Women were sold the waif look of the painfully thin models that adorned the magazines and catwalks. Anorexia, bulimia and other eating disorders spiked as body dysmorphia increased. People chased the pretence that was the perfect body. The irony was that most of these men and women were extremely unhealthy. Models lived on coffee and cigarettes. Bodybuilders cycled steroids, looking shredded for just a few days a year before competitions. Conversely, most firefighters can tell you a story of one of their brothers or sisters who is an absolute workhorse despite being overweight or thin as a rail.

The reality is that fitness is your ability to move efficiently. A side effect is looking good – but it's just that, a byproduct. Chasing a certain body type can lead to some very dangerous training and dietary choices and poor health. Training to move well has the opposite effect. With greater strength, mobility and endurance comes an increased desire to eat cleaner foods, hydrate well and rest appropriately. These in turn lead to a leaner, more muscular frame. I'm pretty sure that the family trapped in the fourth-storey apartment won't want to see your horseshoe triceps before they let you rescue them. Can you do what's asked of you? That is the only true question.

This became clear to me when I reported for my first day at Hialeah Fire Department in 2004. "On your diamond!" the instructor's voice bellowed. Our class of recruits ran to their assigned marks painted on the concrete drill ground, affectionately known as "the Grinder". Three rows of painted diamonds adorned the slab, staggered to give space for the unending calisthenics that awaited us. The instructing cadre consisted of three of the department's best lieutenants, assigned to take our green and just-out-of-the-academy arses and mould us into real-world firefighters. Each one of us had completed EMT school and the appropriately named Minimum Standards to achieve our firefighter certification. The true road to the profession, however, began here.

The basic fire academy had been an amazing experience, fitting it around my full-time office job. I'd been a straight "C" student as a schoolboy yet I found myself excelling there. The application of real-world consequences made sense of the maths, physics, biology and chemistry. I worked out on my lunch break from work and ran several times a week around the Orlando streets. It was an exhausting nine months but also some of the best sleep I've ever had. I watched seemingly ideal candidates fall at the first hurdle and seemingly fragile men and women transform into solid firefighters. We were together four days a week, forming a bond that would last throughout my career and beyond.

And now here I stood, a pasty Englishman in South Florida at the height of summer. It was hot in shorts and t-shirt alone and we had three months in fire gear ahead of us. The morning would begin with an hour of physical training. We ran, performed calisthenics, held traffic cones for weighted exercises, climbed stairs, did pullups and a host of other conditioning movements. With each new week, we added a piece of bunker gear for this PT. The first week was pants, then jacket, then airpack, with the last few weeks of training in full gear, breathing air from the tanks on our backs. This progressive loading worked incredibly well for both strength and heat acclimatisation. Towards the end, we were all doing pullups with thirty pounds of clothing and equipment on our frames.

That was just the first hour. The day then consisted of drilling the skills we would need to perform at the highest level when we hit the streets. We practised ladder throws over and over again. We deployed and reloaded hose. One specific day, we had deployed every single foot of hose from the engine and were diligently reloading it. Each hose had its own specific load. The minute man, triple layer, flat load and horseshoe load, each an orchestration of teamwork as the sun dipped towards the horizon. We neatly folded the last section and stepped down from the rig, tired but content. "Are you missing something?" the instructor shouted. We looked at each other, eyed the folds protruding from the hose beds and shook our heads. "No Sir!" we shouted in unison. He reached into his pocket and held up a black rubber ring. "I disagree!" he bellowed angrily.

We are trained to check for the gasket in the coupling, the rubber seal that ensures the hose doesn't leak at the connections. The instructor had removed one from a section of hose and we hadn't caught it on the reload. Without missing a beat, despite the immense fatigue at the end of a long day in gear, we methodically unloaded the hose until we found and corrected the rogue coupling. What struck me was that there was no blame among us. We had trained together for so long that there was a mutual understanding that we had failed as a team, so we corrected it as a team. I never forgot that lesson, and I checked diligently for gaskets for the rest of my career.

The training was a symbiotic mix of suffering and camaraderie. We were constantly in a place of immense discomfort, slowly learning to tolerate the physical and environmental stresses of the fireground. The burn tower had a chimney that dispersed black smoke and searing heat to all five floors. The fifth floor was incredibly hot, making realistic hose and search evolutions both exhausting and nerve-wracking. We also had a deep understanding of the importance of recovery. These brutal evolutions were followed by appropriate hydration and cooling. We took off our gear and sat in the shade, ice-cold wet towels draped on our heads. Rivers of sweat drained from the doffed bunker gear as it lay in the Florida sun. And then we did it all again.

At the end of the three months, the cadre concocted an unwinnable challenge. The evolution was a multitude of physical and mental tasks designed to find the quitter in us. We were told that if we didn't complete the challenge, our jobs were at stake. That made us dig deep for strength, pushing way past the limits we thought we had reached over the past eleven weeks. I was paired up with my friend Matt. We bunkered up and began the first assignment. In full gear and on air, we had to chop through a wooden telegraph pole with blunt axes. Each strike sent shockwaves through the nylon handle and deep into my bones. The wooden pole seemed to laugh at me, shrugging off my attempts at cleaving it. We took turns hacking at the trunk for eight straight minutes until finally breaking through.

    Matt had barely set the axe down when the instructor shouted, "Fifth floor, highrise strip!" Still in full bunker gear, we ascended the tower, already fatigued from the chopping. Hose and spare air bottles burdened our shoulders, a tool in one hand, railing in the other. I focused on controlling my breathing, air a finite resource on my back. As we crested the staircase, the instructor shouted, "There's a person in the house! Primary search." An initial righthand search for a confirmed victim led us around the fifth floor and down to the fourth floor collapse maze. This labyrinth of wood barely allowed a naked human to pass, never mind one with a fire helmet and air pack. It was designed to scare you, to seek out any weaknesses in your mental resilience and force you to overcome them, or quit.

    "You good?" I asked Matt as we navigated the tunnel. "Right behind you!" he said, voice muffled by the mask as his regulator hissed and heaved with each breath. The maze was pitch black and had a habit of pinching you upside down, inciting panic from deep within. Communication with your partner was imperative to remain calm and keep the creeping fear at bay. We progressed slowly. Matt pushed me through obstacles, then I dragged him through from the other side. Teamwork makes the dream work as they say. The search was exhausting both physically and mentally.

As I rounded the last corner, dim light permeated the cracks of the exit door, a welcome beacon in the unnerving darkness. "We made it!" I called back to him and then dragged his body through the opening, both finally able to stand once more. "Primary search all clear!" I shouted. "Copy that. Follow me," the instructor responded.

The Keiser sled was next, sitting on an outside balcony under the blistering tropical sun. I went first, striking the steel beam repeatedly with an orange nine-pound sledgehammer. I slid backwards with each strike, using bodyweight and leverage to my advantage. The metal I-beam inched along, mocking my fatigued swings. Previously, we would arrive early, sneak up to the sled and clean the track, adding a little oil to make it slide easier. That day, however, it had been deliberately neglected, with rust and sand visibly slowing my progress. Our Vibra-Alerts started chattering, indicating that we were getting low on air. Matt went next, striking the beam back to its original position. His face piece rattled, laboured breaths hissing and rhythmically punctuating the clacking alert system. The steel beam finally reached its home. We quickly changed out bottles, putting new cylinders in our packs, silencing the alarms.

Next up was a ladder evolution. We carried a twenty-four-foot extension ladder around the perimeter of the drill ground before stopping at the building. "There's a victim on the third floor!" the instructor shouted. "Get in there!" We raised the ladder to the rescue position, tied it off and then climbed up. I sounded the floor with my axe and rolled over the windowsill, further checking the floor with stomps of my feet before committing completely. The room was smoked out, with all the other windows closed tightly. As we made it deeper into the structure, visibility diminished to zero. The search took us up and down the building, climbing internal stairs and through furniture-filled rooms. We searched the beds, gently toppled cribs on the off chance an infant was in them. The tower had many closets and cupboards that we could easily have missed if we lost focus.

"I've got a victim!" Matt shouted between breaths. I crawled over to him, feeling the shape of an adult-sized rescue dummy, the heaviest one they had. We fumbled in the dark, strapping webbing around the mannequin to help with the extrication. "Left hand search!" he shouted, and off we went, reversing the route that had got us to that point. The dummy felt much heavier thirty minutes into the simulation. Each corner and step seemed to double its weight. Our breathing grew faster as the exertion increased. "Stay low!" a voice shouted, forcing us down on our knees, an exhausting position to drag from. Matt did an incredible job of navigating, finding an external staircase on which to bring the victim down.

We dragged the dummy onto the concrete below, praying that this was the end. "They need water!" The instructor's voice seemed a thousand miles away. He motioned to the fire engine parked at the side of the building. My eyes were starting to cross with exhaustion, my organs felt like they were cooking in the unbearable heat. Doggedly, we made our way to the back of the rig and picked up the "water thief", a fifty-pound appliance that allows multiple lines to flow off one hydrant. Matt was visibly wobbling, swaying as we carried it over. "Let him do it, Geering!" the instructor screamed, smelling blood in the water. Matt fought valiantly, trying to hold the giant valve up with one hand and connect it with the other. Then he stopped, visibly hitting a physical and mental wall. He placed the water thief on the ground and sank down. "Are you quitting?" the instructor asked. Matt nodded yes weakly.

And in that moment we were done. I would be the world's biggest liar if I said I wasn't equally as ready to tap out. We had worked at full intensity for over fifty-five minutes in bunker gear, under the brutal Miami sun. The heat had sapped every last ounce of energy we had. The moment Matt had metaphorically rung the bell, any semblance of energy I had left vanished. We were ushered to the rehab area and stripped down to shirts and shorts. Ice-cold towels covered our bodies and we drank our weight in watered-down energy drinks. As the day went on, more classmates joined us, all worrying that we had lost our dream jobs by quitting. Some required double IV therapy to stop the excruciating cramping. Others had vomited in their masks while in the maze, breathing through food and bile, unable to remove them until they got out.

As the last group joined us, we found out that all of us had actually passed and that the scenario had been designed for us to fail. It was supposed to take us to a dark place, to set a baseline of discomfort we could reference throughout our careers. The human body is capable of incredible things and we all saw how much further we were able to push. Through a measured balance of extreme work and intelligent cooling and recovery, the instructors had created a cohesive team who were comfortable being uncomfortable. In a career where lives depend on you, the bar must be held high in both fitness and training. This requires the department to value these philosophies and the individuals to have full ownership of their own knowledge and performance. It also needs a trained instructor who understands the importance of athletic rehabilitation.

I cannot think of a better fire department in which to have begun my career. The men and women of Hialeah FD have always held themselves to an incredibly high standard despite falling victim to the city's politics time and again. They've had salaries slashed, pensions cut and almost lost a third of their department (an entire shift) to one mayor's budget cuts. The tactical professions often fall squarely on the financial chopping block, asked to do more with less year upon year. After a national tragedy, they are hailed as heroes, with political figures jockeying for photo opportunities. It doesn't take long for their service and sacrifice to be forgotten before political nominees are selling public service budget cuts to their constituents. What no one mentions is that with budget cuts comes a reduction in service and thus the danger of loss of life.

Firefighters spend years forging their craft. The training is physically brutal, mentally exhausting and performed in gear that is unforgiving to the human body. As with our military special operations community, these tactical athletes require an environment that makes it easy to thrive, yet sadly many are set up for failure. Entry standards are lowered in a misguided attempt to increase recruitment. Annual physical tests are opposed, often by the very unions that are supposed to protect their members. Wellness training and equipment often come at the bottom of the priority list.

How would you feel if your family died because the rescuer hadn't trained? Well, how would you feel? Would you accept that your child perished in a fire because the firefighter was too tired to make it up twenty flights of stairs? Would you accept that your teenage son was shot because the police officer had not learned jiu-jitsu to hone their skills in de-escalation and restraint? Would you accept your wife's death when the paramedic lacked the strength to pull her out of a mass shooting? We rely on these men and women to perform like SAS or Green Berets, but do we train and equip them in the same way? Firefighters are tactical athletes, required to perform incredibly challenging tasks under immense pressure. If strength and conditioning are not given the highest priority, how do we expect the responders to be effective at rescue? Hialeah's academy set the benchmark for my career, and I was constantly looking for ways to improve my fitness and mental toughness. In 2006, I found the answer.

"Do you want to try a workout?" Seven innocent words that have humbled many people across the globe. Neil, my tattoo-covered truck partner had been training in a new gym in Huntington Beach. He had shed several pounds since starting this training and was fitter and stronger than ever. Never one to refuse a challenge, I accepted. He placed a funny-looking object in front of me and said, "We'll do Helen!" Contrary to popular belief, "doing Helen" is not a sexual act but the polar opposite. The weight he gave me looked like a cannonball made for elderly pirates, with an easy-to-grip handle. "Three rounds for time; 400m run, 21 kettlebell swings and 12 pullups," he said with a cheesy grin. "Doesn't sound too bad to me," I replied, grinning back.

In my mind, I was glad it was an easy workout as I had envisioned something far worse. The first round wasn't too bad, my body fresh for each of the three exercises. Then it happened. While running the second lap, an invisible ninja donkey punched me square in my solar plexus. The arid California air refused to enter my lungs, as I trudged down the searing asphalt like a merman that just discovered he had legs. What had happened to my fitness, my pride? I trudged through the next two rounds, gasping like a fish out of water. When the workout was over, I lay on the bay floor in a pool of sweat. "What the bloody hell just happened?" I asked Neil, exhausted and bewildered. This was my introduction to the world of CrossFit.

This training took me to exhaustion in a fraction of the time that my conventional strength and conditioning training as a firefighter and martial artist did. My ego lay bloodied and bruised on the bay floor. I was hooked. This philosophy of high-intensity interval training would carry me through the rest of my career. A few years later CrossFit released a video with its top athletes recalling a near carbon copy of my experience of their first workouts.

Like the proverbial pebble in the pond, this training philosophy was spreading globally. The growth was slow at first. I initially followed the workouts from the CrossFit website. After moving to Ocala, I joined my local YMCA, as there were no CrossFit gyms there at the time. Handstand pushups and double unders would be met by the sneering whispers of the other gym goers, some fast-tracking to become the next orange twins. Fast-forward a couple of years and CrossFit had made the TV and the CrossFit Games were being shown on ESPN. The sneers had been replaced by phrases like "Hey bro, can you show me how to do those muscle ups?" Oh not so funny now, is it mate? CrossFit was suddenly cool with the cut-off muscle-shirt-wearing high-school jocks too.

A strange thing happened to the world of fitness in the middle of the twentieth century. In the 1960s, Joe Weider began to popularise training the physique. The aesthetic aspect of weight training was brought to light, along with an array of bodybuilding machines and supplements. This movement was strengthened when Arnold Schwarzenegger hit the big screen. The bodybuilders of this era relied heavily on free weights and Olympic movements, supplementing their training with specialised machines that were beginning to enter the market. As time went on, these machines began to fill most gyms, and free weights were deemed too dangerous by many risk-management groups.

So why is this an issue? Men and women have been exercising for thousands of years. From the Spartans of ancient Greece to the yogis of India, our ancestors seemed to have a pretty good idea of how to train the human body. In fifty years, these lessons were turned on their head, ignoring millennia of wisdom and experience. Although these new bodybuilding concepts originated from traditional exercises, the advent of machines changed them completely. Where a pullup trained the biceps to work along with all of the stabilising muscles, the preacher curl isolated that muscle, removing nearly all integration. The deadlift is thought to be the king of all weightlifting movements, incorporating most of the body's muscle groups. Conversely, the hamstring curl removed most of the body by lying prone on a bench.

The reason this is an issue for the tactical athlete is the decreased functionality. Don't think for one moment that I am downplaying bodybuilding. It has its place when body sculpture is the goal. Firefighting, however, is a completely different animal. Hoses, ladders and people don't come on a bench with a variety of cams and cables. They are inanimate objects, merciless to the person required to push, pull or lift them. Murphy's Law dictates that the largest of victims will be on the top floor, in the smallest of apartments, crammed into a bathtub or behind a bed. The hose will need to be dragged uphill over a garden full of obstacles. The ladder will need to be thrown by only one firefighter because of staffing constraints.

Just as the Spartans needed to do whatever was required of them, so does the modern-day firefighter. One moment you are doing compressions on a cardiac arrest, hunched over a stretcher in the back of a moving ambulance. The next call you're rappelling over the side of a building and picking off an injured window washer 150 feet in the air. The following call may require donning surface water rescue gear and diving down to a submerged car, fighting fatigue and fear to rescue a trapped driver. The point is that a firefighter's training has to be well rounded to prepare them for the spectrum of potential physical challenges.

So which method is the best? This is where we turn to the "teach a person to fish" philosophy. The mistake many people make is trying to ram one type of exercise down everyone's throats. It's not the exact exercise or routine that matters but understanding the principles behind the appropriate training. A firefighter needs to be strong. The equipment we use is not light and staffing seems to get thinner with each political cycle. More importantly, the firefighter needs to be just as strong twenty minutes into a scene as when they started. Most people can kick in a door, but can you drag your partner out after fighting fire for half an hour? This is the element that is often lost when designing a programme. Three sets on a "pec deck" will most likely fall short for overall conditioning.

There are some in our occupation who won't subscribe to the philosophy that firefighters require an elite level of fitness. I have always compared our profession to that of the secret service agents who protect the President. You would assume that they had seen action on many a battlefield, proving their worth and honing their skills. As the President's bodyguard, the chances of seeing action are now slim and certainly not frequent. This means that these men and women have to train diligently for the one moment they need to perform. This is also true for firefighters, police officers and medics. A majority of emergency calls are relatively mundane and far from challenging. It is easy to get complacent, especially in a quieter station or department.

The very nature of the profession means unpredictability, which draws so many of us in. Not knowing what the next call will be creates a nervous excitement that is absent in most nine-to-five careers. To earn that badge you have to prove that you are prepared to tackle these disasters. We are a Jack of all trades, master of none, but our goal is to be as good as possible at each of them. Like the special operations community, the goal is a high level of proficiency in a range of skills so that we can perform them with reflex-like response. As the saying goes, you fall to your level of training. With that in mind, what is your baseline?

One scenario that illustrates the physical requirement is an explosion in a highrise. Whether deliberate or accidental, this will probably eliminate elevator use. The average firefighter's gear weighs around fifty pounds before they've added any equipment. To fight fire in a highrise, the first crew in must each carry a hose bundle, two spare air bottles and a forcible entry tool. This equates to well over one hundred pounds of equipment, carried up multiple flights of stairs, in gear that won't dissipate any heat. When they reach the fire floor, the firefighters then begin hose deployment and advancement, forcible entry, fire attack, primary search and possibly even victim extrication. Depending on the incident, a victim may need to be carried all the way back down to the ground floor. The victim may then need lifesaving medical interventions, with firefighters using fine motor skills like a cricothyroidotomy or needle thoracotomy.

This scenario is by no means an exaggeration. It was performed by crews at the Alfred P Murrah Federal Building after the Oklahoma City bombing. What is the alternative? That nothing is done? To lose a life because of unpreparedness is unacceptable in our profession. The lowering of physical standards in the first responder community is a dangerous trend, and it's up to the personnel to regulate themselves. If an administration or union blocks a wellness programme or annual fitness tests, it is literally risking the lives of its firefighters and the community they serve. As the saying goes, the more you sweat in peace, the less you bleed in war. So get out there and sweat.

Chapter Three

*Lack of sleep is only bad if you have to drive,
or think, or talk or move.*

– Dov Davidoff

THE TWO-TONE ALARM RIPPED me from a deep sleep. The robotic automated voice followed: "Truck 1, Engine 1, Battalion 1; Fire Response." I felt my mind dragged into consciousness, resistant to the reality that beckoned. The sound of bed covers being ripped back filled the dark bunkroom as I fumbled for my socks. The adrenaline dump catapulted my heart rate, each beat bursting through my chest. I pulled on my socks and grabbed my shirt, throwing it over my head as I navigated the unlit dorm. Casters whirred in their tracks as the doors that protected the pole holes were pulled open. I stood looking down into the abyss as my truck partner Rich slid down the three-storey pole ahead of me. This was a tricky descent when wide awake in daylight. Half asleep at 2am in the pitch black it was a partially controlled freefall into the pad below.

I stepped into my worn leather boots and pulled the bunker pants up, stretching the elasticated braces onto my shoulders. The second repeat came over the loudspeaker: "Apartment complex, flames showing, multiple calls." These magic words told us that this was not a false alarm. This time of night, most residents would be in their homes and fast asleep. The chance of people being trapped by the flames was very high. This is what we trained for. I threw on my bunker jacket and climbed into the doghouse of the tiller truck. Seat belt buckled, I signalled to Joe, my engineer, that I was ready. The Plymovent rails screeched as the truck pulled out of the bay and separated itself from its yellow umbilical cord. As we turned the corner into the street, a familiar yellow glow filled the sky as a column of dark smoke rose through the night air.

Driving the back end of a tiller truck is an art in itself. It defies logic as you initiate turns by steering in the opposite direction. Failure to guide the rear wheels in a smooth arc results in cutting the corner and striking whatever sits on the pavement. I navigated the rear around parked cars and sharp turns while trying to shake off the suffocating fatigue. The dispatcher relayed more information as we grew closer, my mind trying to anticipate what we would need upon arrival. The grinder wailed and the airhorn blasted in the still night as our rig snaked its way through the quiet Anaheim streets. The flashing red lights strobed against the buildings, shadows twisting and turning as we passed.

The structure in question was only four blocks from our station, a mere two minutes' drive in the early morning. We turned onto the street to a three-storey wood-frame apartment building. Flames licked out of the windows and balcony door of two neighbouring apartments on the third floor. Cars were doubled-parked, hindering our access. The tiller's manoeuvrability made it possible to navigate the congested street, missing wing mirrors by mere inches. "Right here, James," Joe said as we came to a halt on the unburned side of the building. Air brakes hissed as he gave me the all-clear through the headset.

I climbed down, opened the gear compartment and swung the airpack onto my back, cinching down the shoulder straps. The axe was next, leather scabbard buckled around my waist. I tugged the airpack's waist straps tight, carrying the weight on my hips and relieving some of the burden on my shoulders. The truck's engine jumped into high idle as the outriggers extended from the truck, reaching for the maximum footprint to stabilise the hundred-foot ladder. I grabbed the steel plate from its shelf, heavy and awkward, and met the outrigger's foot pad, sliding it under to disperse the immense weight. Joe deftly controlled the metal supports, lifting the truck symmetrically to support the cantilever weight of the aerial.

Terry, our captain, walked over to us. He always wore his flash hood en route to the call and looked like an extra from *Monty Python and the Holy Grail* with his bushy ginger moustache protruding from it. "We're going to cut a strip," Terry said. "Yes sir!" we echoed. Terry was economical with his words, trusting our skills, knowing that we had drilled these operations time and again. As we fired up the chainsaws, Joe extended the giant mechanical ladder into the smoky winter night. He set it just above the roofline, no easy feat from his vantage point seventy feet below. We quickly but deliberately climbed the ladder, the low angle rendering the handrail ineffective. I took some deep breaths as each rung took me higher, chainsaw slung over one shoulder, rubbish hook in the opposite hand. The axe handle proved an added hazard, bouncing off the rungs with each step.

Reaching the top, I could see the fire rolling up the opposite side of the building, growing rapidly. I sounded the roof, thumping hard with the hook to ensure it was safe to step onto, then eased my way over, feet feeling for any critical warning signs. Terry and Rich joined me and we fired up the saws. We masked up, the face piece providing protection from both noxious gases and saw debris. I cut an inspection hole, exposing a small section to get a rough idea of the roof construction we would be traversing. This area was notorious for deceptive "reroofs", with multiple layers of material added onto a pre-existing roof. Joe brought more air cylinders up, staging them by the ladder in case we needed to change out.

Rich sounded as we walked, mapping a path of seemingly sturdy structural members. Each of us took care to follow the exact path that was deemed safe by the hook man. We cut indicator holes every ten feet, providing clues as to the fire's direction and intensity. "Here!" Terry shouted through his mask. We formed two teams, as we had so many times before on the drill ground and at previous fires. The saws began to scream as they tore through the shingles and sunk into the plywood below. The thick smoke obscured our vision, hiding the potentially fatal drop beyond.

Sawdust filled the air as we choreographed our cuts. Footwork was precise and deliberate, avoiding the plane of the potentially fatal spinning chain. As the saw man, my cuts had to be surgical, feeling the construction beneath the blade. We rolled rafters to avoid cutting through them and compromising their integrity. The section of roof sagged as the saw completed its final cut. As we pulled back the louvre with the rubbish hook, heavy fire blew out, angry and impatient. We extended the holes to match the intensity of the fire below, increasing the size to maximise the removal of superheated gases. The expanded opening sapped the fire's strength, flames disappearing back into the room.

"We have knockdown," a voice stated on the radio from the engine crew below. This shifted the tactics from an initial attack on the fire to making sure it was completely out. The crew below pulled the ceiling, expanding the makeshift chimney. We pulled out our axes and began overhauling. We pried up shingle, trying to minimise further damage to the roof and eliminate the firefighter's worst nightmare, the rekindle. We cut sections until only clean, unburned lumber remained. "Roof division to command, overhaul complete." It was Terry on the radio, mask hissing between breaths. "Good work, gents!" he said as we weaved our way back to the ladder.

We sounded our way back towards the aerial's quartz light, a halogen beacon in case things had taken a turn for the worse in the thick smoke. Low pressure alarms vibrated as we took off our masks and turned off the bottles. We descended, carrying the tools back to the rig below. We spent the next ten minutes cleaning and refuelling the saws, replacing the now dulled chainsaw chain and replenishing the air in our SCBAs. We sat on the tailboard, drinking water and enjoying the cool air as our core temperature slowly started to normalise. We discussed the call, critiquing our performance and listening to Terry's advice on things we could have done better. I sat there, fully aware of the unique sense of togetherness I was experiencing. We had fought side by side, part of a team of men and women who had saved numerous homes by our proficient and aggressive firefighting.

We spent the next thirty minutes hand-jacking hose, breaking sections and rolling them dry. Tools were hosed off and empty cylinders refilled by the air truck. There's no better feeling of camaraderie than loading hose with brothers and sisters you've just fought fire with. Faces black with soot, shirts drenched with sweat and filthy from shouldering inch-and-three-quarter attack line. The engineers oversaw the hose loads, triple layer here, minute man there, a flat load for the heavy and cumbersome five-inch. And then, after smiles, hugs and pats on the back, the crews climbed into their respective rigs and returned to quarters, knowing they'd made a difference that day.

This isn't a story of heroism or inhuman feats of strength or courage. It's an insight into what firefighters do every day, all around the world. Only five minutes prior to that call I had been in a dead sleep surrounded by my snoring, farting brethren. Minutes later, I was standing on a roof, fifty feet in the air, cutting with a chainsaw as fire licked all around us.

Luckily, on this particular fire there were no victims to find, no dead dogs to bring out to heartbroken children. But still, people's lives had been shattered. Material items like televisions, furniture and toys can be replaced. It's the irreplaceable things that are traumatic. A black-and-white photograph of a relative, a piece of heirloom jewellery or a child's first crayon drawing that was on the family fridge. Some of the most heartrending moments I have seen on a fireground were people digging through charred debris to find a precious locket or a child's piggy bank.

As dawn broke, we wearily drove back to the station to begin the arduous process of thoroughly cleaning hoses and tools. Our gear reeked of the toxic chemicals they had absorbed during the fire, off-gassing into our airways and skin. We needed to clean the turnouts and switch them out with a second set to minimise contact with potentially life-threatening carcinogens. We scrubbed our bodies in piping hot showers in an attempt to remove chemicals from our pores. Blowing our noses revealed a tissue full of black, noxious snot. Then the dispatch message came that we were back in service to do this all over again.

The drive home from a night like this is the next challenge. Many fill themselves to the brim with tar-like firehouse coffee to make it through the commute. Eyelids feel like a thousand pounds as you strain to maintain mental clarity. Windows are down, music is up and the occasional slap to the face maintains consciousness. You finally make it home safely and say a little thank you to your god or the universe. The neighbour from hell starts bitching at you about your rubbish bins not being put away at the correct time. The thought of knocking him out there in the middle of the street is overwhelming. You are spread so thin between mental and physical exhaustion, lack of sleep and the memories you carry from your worst calls. But you find the strength, unfold your fist and just walk away. "It must be nice having so much time off," you hear him mutter as you close the door behind you.

Sleep deprivation is an issue that is rarely, if ever, addressed in the first responder professions. In the fire department, we have become much better at protecting ourselves from hazardous chemicals at fires and other incidents, yet we are still twice as likely as civilians to get certain cancers. When a firefighter gets a horrific disease, we look back to a certain incident and assume a connection. The missing link, the part that is overlooked, is the lack of sleep. A firefighter will lose sleep every night they work for their entire career. Whether they work a twelve-hour nightshift or twenty-four hours at a firehouse, the effects are the same.

Sleep on quieter nights is still of poor quality as the anticipation of a call blocks the ability to fully switch off. The example I always give is this. Imagine you are about to go to sleep and someone stands by your bed holding those giant cymbals used in an orchestra. They tell you that at some point tonight they may or may not smash these things together right by your ears. How well would you sleep? This is the exact "alarm state" that firefighters are in, even if they do get to close their eyes for an hour or two. It's impossible to reach a restorative deep sleep in that state, hence the exhaustion upon waking from a seemingly quiet night.

Dr Kirk Parsley, a retired Navy SEAL turned functional medicine doctor, was finding the same chronic medical conditions in his young and very athletic SEALs. Viewed by many as some of the most elite special forces on the planet, these operators were exercising intensively and eating all of the right foods, yet their blood work was that of men forty years older. It dawned on Dr Parsley that the one common denominator was lack of sleep. Whether going through night training or just extended deployments, the men were coming back in physiological turmoil. He persuaded his command to change the SEALs' work week to allow for more sleep, and within weeks he saw incredible improvement in their overall health. His book *Sleep to Win* is an invaluable resource.

Unlike most professions, first responders don't know what a call is going to entail until it happens. For firefighters it could be a fire, traffic collision, rope rescue, marine rescue or some other emergency that no one else is trained for. A police officer may be involved in a car chase, foot pursuit, fight or gun battle. The paramedic may roll up on an active shooting or explosion. The zero to a hundred nature of our professions takes a huge toll on the human body. This adrenal fatigue, the constant stress of expecting the worst-case scenario, prevents the body from repairing and growing. The fight or flight response is a primitive mechanism designed to keep us safe, but historically the danger was short lived. That meant that the body could then return to a relaxed "parasympathetic" state.

The problem is that the same mechanism can kill us if it never turns off. Stress keeps this sympathetic nervous system ticking over and doesn't allow the parasympathetic state (feed and breed) to kick in and start repairing all of the damage from the previous day. This is exacerbated by lack of sleep. Night-time is when the body repairs injury and grows muscle. In order to do this, the sympathetic nervous system has to be turned off to allow the parasympathetic system to begin the healing process. By missing one night of sleep, your body's hormones become completely imbalanced. Testosterone is halved, blood sugar rises and you have the same neurological function as with a blood alcohol level of 0.1%, which is well over the legal limit.

Another element of sleep that has often been thought of as fallacy is sleep debt. In his book *The Promise of Sleep*, Dr William Dement details how sleep debt is in fact a very true phenomenon, but it's not known how long this debt lasts. He verified that the average person needs either side of eight hours' sleep every night to perform optimally. Therefore, just one night without sleep immediately puts you eight hours in debt. Multiply this by a career of 20 to 30 years and you have a huge health problem. Naps can certainly help but they are no substitute for deep, restorative sleep.

The immune system cannot function well in this deprived state, putting the first responder at a much greater risk of autoimmune disease and cancer, and cancer is the primary physiological killer in our profession. With the resulting hormonal imbalance, weight gain often follows, turning once svelte first responders into deconditioned versions of their former selves. Wrought with hypertension and type II diabetes, responders are now typically at high risk of heart disease, the second-highest killer in our profession. Testosterone plummets with shift work, affecting libido, work capacity and muscle growth. Muscles and connective tissue repair in the deep sleep phase. By repeatedly losing sleep, injury becomes a foregone conclusion. A physically active firefighter requires even more sleep to repair, which is why the fittest of them are often more prone to injury if constantly sleep deprived.

The brain is not spared from this destructive sleep behaviour. It has been shown that sleep deprivation mimics traumatic brain injury; the same injury attributed to depression and suicide among soldiers, football players and combat athletes. Once again, the hormonal disruption affects the brain's chemistry and is directly linked to mental ill health. As with the body, the brain processes and repairs during the sleep phases. Sleep deprivation causes the pancreas to malfunction, creating yet another risk factor for metabolic-related disease. Parkinson's disease is now being referred to as type III diabetes, suggesting that it is actually preventable. I am convinced that sleep, and therefore recovery, is one of the missing pieces in the treatment of PTSD and associated mental health conditions.

So what is the answer? Certainly, eliminating shift schedules is not the solution. The bottom line is that someone has to work at night to protect the citizens we serve. Someone has to climb that ladder to reach the trapped victim or arrest the violent husband before he murders his estranged wife. The answer is twofold.

Firstly, the first responder's work week needs to be reduced – and yes, that means more personnel, but that's the price of effectively protecting a community. A fifty-six-hour work week with no sleep is a recipe for disaster. Responders need time to recover from these shifts and catch up on sleep debt. Naps should be encouraged, not banned, to allow some rest. Would you want the person driving your child to hospital in an ambulance to be functioning at the level of a drunk driver?

Investing in people and valuing human life should be enough to persuade cities or counties to increase staffing. Sadly, these factors don't seem to hold much weight in government. So here's the fiscally sound argument. Running departments with a skeleton crew is a false economy. Short term, it may make the current administrator look great, securing them a nice Christmas bonus for cutting the budget. However, if you crunch the numbers, the long-term cost is far greater. When first responders get sick or die, it's expensive. Worker insurance is expensive, medical retirements are expensive. Wrongful death lawsuits are extremely expensive.

When a responder is sleep deprived, the likelihood of mistakes grows exponentially. Knowing that cognitive function is greatly reduced, how many line-of-duty or citizen deaths have been caused by this phenomenon? The paramedic who misdiagnosed chest pain? The police officer who blew through a red light killing a family of four? The firefighter who fell from the aerial after missing a step onto the building? Add together the end-of-career payouts and you see where the shortsightedness costs the employer dearly. High-level sports athletes and special operations warriors have teams of experts behind them, ensuring they receive adequate rest to maximise performance. Airlines, the trucking industry, the naval fleets all have mandated sleep. The Chernobyl, Exxon Valdez and space shuttle Challenger disasters all had sleep deprivation listed as a significant contributing factor. Still think your plan is financially sound?

Secondly, individuals need to take ownership of the problem. The first responder professions are often woefully underpaid, forcing many into a second job to buffer income. Taking a night shift at an ER or riding a private ambulance through the night is going to compound the sleep problem. Overtime is another culprit. I'm often told that creating a shorter work week will only encourage more overtime. I disagree. An understaffed fire department causes more overtime, as workers are forced to stay an additional twenty-four hours. By investing in the department, overtime spots cease to be a perpetual opportunity, thus reducing the likelihood of burnout. If a second job involves a hard day's work followed by sleep in their own bed, the chance of recovery is far greater.

If you are working in the profession, you need to be your own advocate. You need to practise good sleep hygiene at home. That means being strict with yourself about going to bed early. Black out your bedroom as light is a cue for alertness and can prevent you entering deep sleep. Turn down the air. The optimal temperature is around 67 degrees. Although this may sound cold, it is widely accepted in the sleep medicine world. To wind down, turn off devices and consider reading or even doing some gentle yoga or mindfulness practice before bed. There are some incredible apps now that guide you through a ten-minute meditation, which is also a great way to decompress after a stressful call. Try to avoid alcohol in the evening as it will also prevent getting into deep restorative sleep, causing that all too familiar brain fog the next day. You have an opportunity to make a huge difference to your own mental and physical health. Sleep deprivation needs to be talked about as its physical and mental effects are devastating. You are an athlete, so start treating yourself as one.

Chapter Four

People readily demonstrate their willingness to sacrifice their safety and survival for the sake of something beyond themselves, such as family, country or justice.

– Atul Gawande

The alarm goes off, a seemingly harmless ringtone on my phone that now grinds to the very core of my soul. The obnoxious tune snatches me from a deep sleep. It's 5am, only six hours since I was able to lie down in my own bed. I scramble for the phone to turn off the grating sound before it wakes my wife. She stirs slightly, then rolls to the other side, unphased. Years of this routine have dulled her response. I look at her for a moment, the woman who stole my heart on our very first date. Her petite frame covered by the ornate brown duvet, gentle features barely visible in the near darkness. My brain interrupts this moment of adoration as my monkey mind begins Einsteinesque equations. How long did I sleep? What do I have to do today? What is the magnesium sulphate dose for eclampsia?

    I push the covers off and swing my legs over the edge. I take a moment to say a little prayer of gratitude, something I learned from the late Wayne Dyer. Beginning the day with a thank you calibrates everything else that happens. Thank you for my family's health. Thank you for our home, food and clothes. Thank you for the opportunity to make someone's life better today. I walk over to the bathroom and gently close the door before turning on the light. This choreographed routine is essential to minimise the chance of waking the rest of the household. As the shower heats up, I stare at my reflection in the mirror. The face that stares back is old and tired, marred by deep lines. Eyes that hold images most will never see, surrounded by dark circles marking decades of sleepless nights.

Random thoughts insult my weary mind as I stand motionless in the shower, water gently massaging my sore shoulders. I feel the stiffness from last night's workout, torn calluses stinging from the soap lathering in my hands. I realise that for the past fourteen years I've woken up next to my wife only one out of every three days, had breakfast with my son for just a third of his life. A sobering thought. The introspection then shifts to how easy life might be if I turned to a nine-to-five desk job, getting to come home every night to be with my family and sleep in my own bed. Then I laugh and remind myself that I would have strangled someone by the end of my first day in a cubicle.

I creep around the house, packing the multiple bags required for a twenty-four hour shift. My German shepherd's tag clinks and her feet tip tap on the wooden floor, thwarting my efforts at stealth. I pack several uniforms in case I get vomited on by an overdose patient, climb down an elevator shaft or have to load soot-covered hose back onto the engine. I need gym gear too to make sure I get the all-important workout done. Computer bag is next, ensuring I have all of the hardware and books for the neverending education of a modern-day firefighter or paramedic. Finally, bags of food to cover twenty-four hours, with the potential of being forced to hold over for the following shift.

I quietly open Tai's bedroom door, the motion sensor setting off the night light, which gently illuminates his face. He's starfished, limbs hanging off the bed, blanket balled up at his feet. Gently, I unfurl the cover and lay it back over him. "I love you," I whisper. I say a silent blessing and close the door. Ethan, my bonus boy, lies sleeping in the next room; another prayer from outside his door. I return to our bedroom and kiss Becky goodbye, again whispering "I love you", not knowing if this will be the last time I ever get to say those words. I hate leaving them; it never gets easier.

My commute to the station is exactly seventy-five minutes if there is no traffic. I listen to a podcast to educate myself and make the most of the extended journey. In my mind, the goal is to arrive at the station slightly more intelligent than when I left my home. I pay multiple tolls, spending an average of fifteen dollars every time I drive to and from my second home. The roads are quiet, making the commute somewhat enjoyable. A strong cup of coffee helps combat the fatigue compounded by the monotony of motorway driving. I get to the station half an hour early to ensure my colleagues can avoid a last-minute call and get home to their families. Then the day begins, checking out gear, running tools and inventorying medical equipment, trying to prepare for whatever the universe may throw at us today.

To some, the badge on our chest is a piece of metal that is given when we're hired by a department. To the rest of us, it represents the honour of protecting our community. It's a symbol of sacrifice by the wearer and respect for the citizens that we serve. This respect is not handed out like some flyer for a new restaurant in a busy high street. Being a first responder demands a pledge, to be the best version of yourself and to protect your community. The shield represents the professionalism we have trained diligently to earn. We have learned to thrive in high-stress environments, keeping emotions and actions separate.

So, ask yourself this: What is your why? Why do you wake up in the morning? What do you hope to have achieved by the time your head hits the pillow at the end of the day? In a world where a day can comprise video games, social media and reality television, these are very powerful questions. Knowing your why is fundamental to excelling in every aspect of your life. What kind of life do you want to live and what impact do you want to have on the world? If you are a first responder, what was the fire that was burning inside when you made the decision to apply to fire academy, police academy or paramedic school? What did you dream of doing once you passed the state test and were finally wearing the uniform you'd envisioned yourself in?

This burning desire is what gets me up at the crack of dawn and tears me away from my family for a relatively small salary. My desire has always been to serve my community, to be there when people are having their worst day. There seems to be a commonly held delusion that a country is made great by its leaders. Forgive me if I disagree, but I believe it's the men and women who serve their communities that are the backbone of nations around the globe. The common denominator in all religious scriptures is to serve others with kindness and compassion. This basic human desire to help others has been demonstrated many times. From the New Yorkers of 9/11 to the Londoners of 7/7, people have found incredible compassion and courage in times of tragedy.

The "why" also drives all other aspects of our life. If you have a passion to serve, then you also have a desire to be the best damn firefighter, police officer or EMT you can possibly be. This involves training both your body and mind. This passion is what gets you off your arse and into the gym, forging your body into an efficient machine. The average first responder's career will span twenty-five years and there is no excuse for not being able to do the job right up until the last day. The fifty-year-old veteran should be a leader both physically and mentally, ready to teach the rookie how to stay alive in this dangerous profession.

We need to apply the same aggressive attitude to the skills we are responsible for. Whether subduing a combative felon, cutting a trench on a burning five-storey apartment complex or suctioning a newborn's airway, these skills need practice. Without ownership by both departments and individuals, people will die. Innocent civilians get shot by badly trained police officers. Prison inmates die at the hands of overly aggressive guards. Elderly patients succumb to the actions of a paramedic who pushed the wrong drug. A child dies in a blaze because a firefighter had a panic attack wearing a mask. These deaths are both preventable and unacceptable.

To perform at a high level as a first responder, we have to view ourselves as tactical athletes. We need a team the same way a martial arts fighter or ice hockey player does. Most of us are required to work through the night when the average citizen is sleeping. This constant sleep deprivation means that we have to strengthen the pillars of health that are in our control to offset the damage from shift work. Nutrition is an area that can make or break us, creating a strong base or an unstable structure just ready to collapse. We can mitigate stress levels through some sort of mindfulness practice, whether meditation, art or fishing. Clearing the mind of the white noise of everyday life creates a calm that resets the stress level. The scenes we are exposed to can crush the mind if this self-care is not reinforced.

Physical training is where the "why" truly comes into its own. It takes a lot of self-discipline and motivation to push yourself to the edge in your training. We have to be able to keep going when the average person would have thrown in the towel. Mental toughness is imperative when lives are at stake. Training includes stress inoculation, creating physically exhausting scenarios that test us mentally to ensure we can perform when we are needed the most. The person needing rescue doesn't care if you are tired, hot or bleeding. There are only two outcomes, success or failure, and the latter is not an option. Reminding ourselves of why we chose this profession is what drives us through the pain cave, the unbearable suffering of the red line.

Bullfighter Juan Belmonte was quoted as saying, "No life worthy of the name consists of anything more than the continual series of struggles to develop one's character through the medium of whatever one has chosen as a career". I couldn't agree more.

Although our own sacrifice is ever apparent, the unsung heroes of the first responder and military professions are the families. Husbands and wives in effect become single parents when their loved ones are on shift or deployed. For days, weeks or even months they have to be both parents while praying their loved one will return. There is no other spouse or partner to hand the screaming baby to. No one else to clean up the half-eaten squirrel the dog vomited up in the living room. They sleep alone, in a bed made for two, without the protection of their loved one. The children see other parents coaching their football team and attending events at school, but not their own. Holidays are fluid, celebrating Christmas on whichever day mum or dad can be physically at home. The family endures hurricanes, tornadoes and wildfires alone as their beloved firefighter, police officer or medic deploys into the community they serve.

Another cost surfaces when we return home. If we don't acknowledge the burden our family endures, it can be a recipe for disaster. Yes, we may have had a stressful shift both physically and mentally. Our family, however, may have endured their own stressors and be in need of comfort, affection or simply a break. It is important that we separate the responder role from the family role. Bringing the trauma home without decompressing only compounds the situation. Some days we may need additional support from our families. On others, they may need to lean on us. Life does not stop just because we went to work.

The mental and physical challenges of the first responder professions often bleed into marriages and relationships. The extreme fatigue and emotional burden have tragically destroyed many families. While this is far from a foregone conclusion, it can't be ignored. Success in the fire service requires a strong family unit. When this structure is weakened through a lack of compassion on either side, collapse is a definite threat. I hold the men and women I've worked alongside as some of the best parents out there. The desire to serve others is coupled with the kindness required as a doting mother or father. It breaks my heart when I see the toll of shift work begin to strain what was once a beautiful love story. We need to take ownership of the mental health of ourselves and the ones we love. Disregarding post-traumatic stress, addiction and burnout can have catastrophic consequences.

We have been blessed with the amazing opportunity to wear the badge, tasked with protecting and rescuing those who are unable to do so themselves. Mother Theresa once said, "If you want to change the world, go home and love your family." That's what drives me to train diligently, exercise vigorously, read voraciously and rest intelligently. I have a responsibility to come home to those I adore: my wife, children and German shepherd. They are my why. What's yours?

Chapter Five

Our human compassion binds us, the one to the other, not in pity or patronizingly, but as human beings who have learnt how to turn our common suffering into hope for the future.

– Nelson Mandela

"She fell again." The elderly man was standing at the open door, one hand on the handle, the other leaning into a dark wooden cane. He had an emerald-green dressing gown draped over his thin frame as if on a wooden hanger. He was clearly upset, his face a mix of helplessness and shame. "I'm sorry we called you gentlemen so late." As we walked into his home, Terry assured him it was no trouble at all. The man had clearly struggled with the decision to call 911, pride visibly wounded. It was 3am and the city of Anaheim was sleeping, oblivious to this one household's turmoil. We set down the medical box, airway bag and monitor we had brought in case this wasn't simply a citizen assist.

A faint moan echoed from the back of the house, amplified by the mahogany floors and wall panelling.

"She's in the bedroom." We made our way through the narrow hallway of the ranch-style home. Black-and-white pictures adorned the panels, spanning its length. "I couldn't pick her up," the man said, shuffling slowly behind us, sad frustration evident in his weary voice. As we entered the bedroom, an elderly woman lay face up on the carpeted floor. Her head was craned awkwardly against the bedside table, eyes red from tears, further magnified by her white nightgown. A framed photograph lay face down on the floor next to her. I picked it up and returned it to what appeared to be its original position on the nightstand.

In the photo were a young man and woman. The man wore a US Army uniform, hat cocked slightly to the side. A cigarette hung loosely from the corner of his mouth, framed by his Clark Gable-style moustache. He had the physique of an athlete and would not have looked out of place in a wartime boxing ring. The woman in the picture was petite, hair curled beneath a 1940s hat. She wore a white blouse tucked into a heavily pleated grey skirt. They were holding hands, looking lovingly at each other. They reminded me of the faded pictures of my grandparents during wartime.

I could still see the resemblance in the elderly woman's face, despite the embarrassment and discomfort that distorted it. She looked at us, desperation visible in her eyes.

"I'm so sorry!" she apologised. "I'm such a nuisance!"

"I couldn't disagree more," I replied. "This is exactly what we're paid to do. Does anything hurt at the moment?"

"No," she responded. "I was trying to get out of bed to use the commode but my legs gave way again."

I assessed her for injuries then Rich and I gently lifted her up and sat her on the bed. "Do you still need to go to the bathroom?"

"Yes," she replied as her embarrassment returned. "I think I may have soiled myself."

We take so much for granted in life. The simple act of standing, walking and using the toilet barely enters our mind. This once innate action had now become immeasurably challenging for this woman. After escorting her to the privacy of her bathroom, we removed her soiled underwear and cleaned her up. As a rookie, I had no idea of the impact of simply restoring someone's dignity, the power of a simple change of clothes.

Her feeling of helplessness soon dissolved as we walked her back into the bedroom. We helped her back into bed and checked her again to be sure no new ailments were evident. "Thank you so much, gentlemen!" she said. "I'm sorry to be so much trouble."

We assured her again that it was our duty to help when needed. "Please don't hesitate to call us again if you need us," I said with a smile.

As we walked back into the living room, we had time to look a little closer at the photographs. The same young man in the bedroom photograph stood grinning ear to ear, one hand on his Curtiss P-40 Warhawk, the other on his hip. The plane was adorned with shark-like teeth and scowling cartoon eyes. I can't imagine what the enemy pilots must have thought when they saw that caricature face bearing down on them. "That was taken three weeks before the Japanese bombed us."

The frail man who had struggled to open his own front door was once a USAAF fighter pilot, stationed at Pearl Harbor. He was one of the only men to get their planes into the sky during the attack, shooting down two enemy aircraft. His wife had been in the Army Nurse Corps, also stationed in Hawaii. In an instant, their hospital had gone from administering physicals and vaccinations to being an emergency trauma centre.

"That's where we met," he said, smiling for the first time. "My best friend had been wounded by one of the bombs. I finally got to visit him in the hospital and there was this angel taking care of him. It was love at first sight." The smile grew as he recounted his chance meeting. "We were married six months later, and have spent sixty-five years together. She's my best friend." He stayed looking at the picture, as if reliving that very moment, then turned back to us. "Thank you again. You have no idea what it means to me," and he wiped a tear from his eye.

"We should be thanking you," I replied. "I hope we can make even a fraction of an impact on the world that you both have." We said our goodbyes, picked up our equipment and left.

They had been involved in one of the biggest tragedies in US history. As the harbour was attacked, they had been protecting and treating their fellow Americans. Fast-forward to our call and he didn't even have the strength to pick his wife off the floor. I can't imagine what that must be like, to physically not be able to protect the woman who stole your heart. To go from fighting for your country to feeling deeply vulnerable.

These "back to bed" calls were always some of my favourites. It was moving to see a crew could show up at a home with the muscle to undo whatever misfortune had befallen the resident. Sometimes it would just need a lift back into a chair or bed. There were other times where the resident was so incontinent that we had to give them a shower. Of course, this is not the most pleasant thing for a responder to have to do, but the reward far outweighs the brief moment of discomfort. There is an irony in the fact that firefighters are often disciplined for not abiding firmly by standard operating procedures. Some have made heroic rescues only to face disciplinary action. Cleaning a patient up is not in our job description but we do it from a place of compassion. Sometimes these lines are blurred and the core of public service is lost. We are there to mitigate someone's emergency, whether pulling them from a fire or just back up off the floor.

When we talk about prejudice in our society, the focus is usually on race, religion or sexual orientation. Unlike many of the world's tribes, our elders are held in disdain in many circles, as if a lifetime of service is suddenly nullified once grey hair and wrinkles set in. How many people walked past our frail couple with no idea of the sacrifice they both made for America? The world is full of people who have done incredible things for their communities. Firefighters who were at the 1942 Coconut Grove Nightclub incident, which claimed 492 lives. Police officers who responded to the 1963 bombing in Birmingham, AL. Scientists who contributed to the first space launch. Teachers who inspired the men and women we revere today. Greatness surrounds us, disguised as "old people". Sadly, kindness can get lost in this profession, a form of compassion fatigue eating away at the good in a person. I was to see its ugly head raised during my formative days in the fire service.

It was one of the very first calls of my career. The deafening tone that caused an instant adrenaline rush was followed by a muffled, monotone voice. "Person down," said the dispatcher. There was an immediate response from the men on my crew that day, a chorus of groans and eye-rolling. I wondered how two short words could create such disdain. "This is going to be bullshit!" one of the firefighters exclaimed as he skulked out into the bay. I wondered if he'd had these fortune-telling skills since birth or whether a science experiment had gone horribly wrong. We jumped into the engine and drove to the location.

Upon arrival, a small-framed man was lying prone on the pavement. Two police officers were already on scene and my crew stepped up to join them. "Oh, surprise, surprise! Another bum!" I heard one of them mumble. One of the police officers continuously pushed the man with her foot, shouting, "Hey, buddy! Get up! Get up!" The man was unable to get up, clearly unconscious and unaware of our presence. Despite being a brand new rookie, I'd had enough of the way the call was going. I decided to initiate an assessment, as no one else had even checked to see if he was breathing. After establishing that his vitals were within normal limits, I began to search his pockets to look for clues as to his identity and medical history.

My hand found a piece of paper, which I pulled out and unfolded. It was from a lab and showed the results of a recent blood test. The man had just learned that he was HIV positive. I'm pretty sure that every judgemental person on that scene would most likely have got drunk too after hearing that kind of news. This man was lying on the side of the road, having received a death sentence, and the men and women he paid to protect him were treating him like some sort of subhuman scum. Now let me point out that this is one of the absolute lows of my career and is far from the norm with most fire, police and EMS crews. It was the perfect storm of disgruntled people having a bad day.

I have worked in some of the most disadvantaged neighbourhoods on the east and west coasts. The people who walk the streets range anywhere from angels to demons and everywhere in between, but they are all still people. Most first responders have walked into a filthy crack den with expensive cars in the driveway and children running around in filthy clothes and with empty stomachs. There is no doubt that some kids are set up for failure, an uphill battle from birth. We are blessed if we've been raised by parents who gave us the tools and confidence to follow our dreams and serve our communities. The less fortunate people we see didn't dream of becoming drug addicts, being homeless or turning to prostitution. They are our most desperate brothers and sisters, victims of a twist of fate or just poor life decisions.

Our society is suffering from a malignant cancer in the form of selfishness and an absence of compassion. There are of course many people who don't fit this mould, but there has been something missing in society over the past few decades that has hurt us, not just in our community but in our profession. The compassion for our fellow citizens has been dampened by news stories of welfare abuse and greedy corporation fraud. We are raised in a competitive society where you must "destroy the opposition" and be victorious. This has bled into the first responder arena, where burned-out firefighters, paramedics and police officers have become numb to the suffering. In its extreme, this can lead to tragic deaths like that of thirteen-year-old Drew Hughes, killed by a series of medical malpractices, and the murder of George Floyd.

I hope you understand this is not me standing in a glass house throwing stones. I constantly have to check my own heightened sense of self-importance. I wear the badge of a profession that is pretty well respected by complete strangers, and it has an allure of power. What I love about the fire service is that mostly, when it hits the fan, there is no prejudice, whether cultural, racial or socioeconomic. A person in need is a person in need and we are there to make their worst day a little better. The job undoubtedly creates mental and physical fatigue and we all have our bad days. What makes us professionals is that we have the discipline to rise above our emotions when spat on or when we take the brunt of racial slurs.

Historically, tragedy has brought people together and has created the much-needed tribe effect that is often missing in our culture these days. The London bombings, 9/11 and the Pulse shooting are just a few of the horrific events that have bonded communities, overcoming cultural bias. To me, that is the true essence of humanity. We signed up for fire academy, medic school or police academy so we can help people. Renowned holistic farmer Joel Salatin once said, "First responders are at the fringe of society." He is right. We see the holes in the fabric of our community. This goes both ways though and we can both inspire and infuriate the people that we serve. I truly believe that we have the power to help our neighbours rediscover their humanity, compassion and sense of community.

Most people are yearning for a sense of tribe in modern society, and this couldn't be more apparent than in the isolation of the Covid-19 pandemic, which is affecting us all as I write this. I believe this search for tribe is the underlying reason why team activities like CrossFit and obstacle races are so popular. Deep down, people are good and want to do good for others. For first responders, this is one of the key ingredients to good mental health. Nothing feels better than helping another human being and expecting nothing in return. I am proud to wear my badge and stand side by side with like-minded first responders around the globe. We are role models, whether we like it or not, and our actions are magnified in the eyes of those who look up to us. All religious doctrines teach compassion and it has been practised for centuries by their prophets, showing us by example how to follow. We have a responsibility to be the person that our community thinks we are. We can truly affect our countries for the better if we hold ourselves to the same high standard.

I want to tell you another story to illustrate the inherent good in people. John sat on the couch, nasal cannula gently hissing, snaking from his nose to the oxygen machine in the hallway. His eyes were tired, with deep rings surrounding them, attesting to the battle that had been raging in his body for the past three years. Emotion was gone from his face, replaced with a perpetual look of exhaustion. A purple crocheted blanket lay over his lap, and he was proudly wearing his grey Orange County Fire Rescue shirt. The room was full of his closest friends and family, there to share this powerful moment with him. The tragic mix of sadness and love was palpable, knowing this could be the last time many would see him.

John had been in the fire service for decades. He started as a wildland firefighter in California, entering through a troubled youth programme at the age of eighteen. After moving to Florida, he spent fifteen years as an Orange County firefighter, most of them on the prestigious special operations team. He was the station joker, the life of the party and a damn good firefighter. Around ten years into his career, John started experiencing periods of extreme fatigue. He sought medical advice and was diagnosed with a rare autoimmune disease. He slowly deteriorated, ultimately having to retire from the profession he loved so much.

One of John's wishes was to watch the film *Only the Brave*, which was just about to be released in the cinemas. His fragility rendered him unable to travel or be around large groups of people and he was resigned to the fact that he wouldn't be able to see the film before he died. The film tells the story of the Prescott 19, the Granite Mountain Hotshots tragically killed in the 2013 Yarnell wildfire. I had been fortunate to interview Amanda Marsh, the widow of Superintendent Eric Marsh, who was portrayed so powerfully by Josh Brolin. Brendan McDonough, the lone survivor of the crew, who was a lookout on another ridge, was also on my podcast, as was Josh himself.

John's wife, Rachel, had asked if I could think of any way of facilitating a viewing for John. I reached out to Sony Pictures, who were distributing the film. Without hesitation they volunteered to fly a hard copy of the film two and a half thousand miles from Los Angeles to Fort Lauderdale. Michelle, one of Sony's representatives, then drove two hundred miles north to Orlando. When she arrived, we helped her hook the hard drive to the television and arranged every chair and stool we could find.

Then it began, a bear, engulfed in fire, running out of the woods in slow motion. I glanced at John periodically, watching his face reliving his wildland days. The little movement the disease allowed him showed subtle hints of the joy and sadness he experienced as the story unfolded on the screen. We laughed at the trash talking between the Hotshots, relating it to our own firehouse experiences. We watched in admiration as Eric led his men in training and on the fireground. We all cried together as Brendan found out his entire crew had been killed and Amanda learned that the sole survivor wasn't Eric. The story of one of the biggest tragedies in US wildland firefighting history was told so beautifully, drawing the entire room through a spectrum of emotions.

John dried his eyes and gave his wife and daughter a hug. "Thank you!" he said to Michelle, embracing her, tears streaming down his cheeks. Then he started to recall stories from his wildfire days. His face lit up as his memory put him back on a Californian mountain in yellow Nomex and thick-heeled leather boots. The mental journey then travelled east as his crew recounted John's numerous firehouse pranks and hilarious behaviour. He was truly a vibrant and positive soul and such a passionate firefighter. Although there were so many stories left untold, it became clear that John was exhausted. The brotherhood and sisterhood in that room was incredibly powerful. Firefighters, spouses, daughters and a kind-hearted woman who drove four hundred miles for a complete stranger. Two short weeks after we shared that incredible moment, John passed away.

The news outlets and social media feeds love to display a smorgasbord of misery and division to the masses. When you pull back the curtain of "Oz", you realise that this is just what they want you to see, not the truth. People are inherently good and often just need to be led in the right direction. A simple act of kindness can change someone's day or even life. As a responder, you may pull someone out of a house fire or simply be the first person who showed someone compassion in a long time. Whether it's an elderly widow living in a care home or a homeless addict living under a bridge, kindness can change someone's world. We are taught a multitude of lifesaving skills, but kindness and compassion are our most powerful tools. Never let them dull.

Chapter Six

Power is no blessing in itself, except
when it is used to protect the innocent.

– Jonathan Swift

It was a beautiful sunny Florida day as I drove my son back to school after his annual wellness check. Tai sat there, chewing on the lolliop the doctor had given him after another clean bill of health. The paediatrician was a kind man with an incredible gift for interacting with children. At ten years old, Tai still giggled when the doctor told him he was looking for French fries between his ears, as he peered through the otoscope. We reflected on his visit as he thanked God for another year with no shots. Even the occasional wheezing he was prone to had ceased since he started taking CBD, the non-psychotropic element of hemp.

In the street that leads up to his elementary school, I saw several sheriff's vehicles tearing down the road in the opposite direction. Assuming they had been called to an incident in town, I continued to the school. We walked across the car park and into the building as we had hundreds of times before. As I approached the front desk, doctor's note in hand, a teacher shouted "Code Red!" Adults immediately began shepherding children into classrooms and I heard the doors being locked behind me. "You're going to have to come into the supply room with us, Mr Geering!" one of the teachers exclaimed. The school alarm started, a metallic screeching reminiscent of a 1990s video game. "Attention! Lockdown! Lockdown! Lock the doors! Stay away from the windows!" the robotic voice commanded, over and over again.

I recognised the term Code Red from discussions with Tai. He had recounted on several occasions that the school ran drills "in case a bad guy tries to shoot us", as he put it. Hearing this would put my heart firmly in my throat as images from the Sandy Hook Elementary massacre flashed in my head. I use the word massacre deliberately, as people these days often seem to downplay the horror, with words such as "active shooter" or "act of terror". Tai would explain the way he and his classmates practised sheltering in place. I felt a deep sense of sadness that innocent children, whose only concern should be which game to play next, had to drill for their own potential murder.

The room we sheltered in was where the printers and paper products were stored. Most of the kids and staff were hiding in their classrooms or under dinner tables, caught having lunch in the cafeteria. It was then that it struck me just how vulnerable these children and their guardians are. Had an armed assailant entered the building, he (I say that as they are nearly always male) would have met minimal resistance. I looked around the room and identified objects that could be used as a weapon. A fire extinguisher hung from the wall, cumbersome but a possible distraction. On the table by the printer was a paper guillotine. Upon closer examination, ripping the handle off would have created a pretty effective machete. My mind raced with all of the potential entry points a motivated shooter could exploit.

The teachers I shared the small space with frantically searched the internet on their phones, trying desperately to find some clues as to what was happening. What you underestimate as a spectator is just how disconnected the people inside a school are from what everyone outside knows. I was so impressed with how quickly the staff had corralled the children into their various shelters, and you could literally have heard a pin drop during the incident. Although the light was off in our room, the entrance area outside was still illuminated by the large windows and double glass doors.

Tai turned to me and said, "I'm so glad you're here with me, Daddy." At that moment, it hit me that the other little girls and boys were hiding under desks in total darkness, terrified, not knowing if they were going to see their parents again. "At least there is a paramedic here with us," he continued. "You can help people if the bad guy shoots them." At that moment, I realised that I was there under many banners. Of course, as a firefighter and paramedic, I had already sworn an oath to protect the people I was sharing the building with. The other side, though, was that I was there as his dad.

I am not a soldier or a police officer, but if someone had entered with a weapon, there was no question that I was going to stop them or die trying. This is not fake machismo; it would have been terrifying. But at that point I was my son's protector, and there was no time to turn back the clock. Whatever I had done up to that point was the sum total of my training. Had I spent the previous twenty years on a couch, the chances of being able to protect my son and his friends would have been slim to none. As a lifelong martial artist, first responder and athlete, those chances were significantly higher.

As it happened, this Code Red, the first one in the school's history, was a false alarm. There was a report of a threat towards one of the student's parents and the assailant had stated he was coming for her child too. The local law enforcement agency had done a great job of taking the threat seriously and acted accordingly.

In the fire department we call this a "near miss". There are two ways of reacting. Either do absolutely nothing and therefore learn absolutely nothing, or use it as an opportunity to learn and grow. False alarms and near misses are a gift allowing you to save lives if the event ever happens again but with more deadly results. To ignore such an event and nurture the complacency that is the cancer of many departments is unacceptable.

As I sat there in that school, I gained a soul-shaking insight into the potential disaster that could have followed. So what did I learn when I was standing in the supply room and scanning for weapons like some warped episode of *The Walking Dead*? Had this been a true threat, the incident would have had one of two outcomes based on who responded.

Scenario one: The deputies, firefighters and medics who show up have taken their jobs seriously every day of their careers, and as a result they save many lives. The law enforcement officers have gone outside of their agencies and taken tactical shooting courses. These have prepared them with military-level tactics, enhancing their effectiveness and increasing their own safety. The paramedics have also taken a tactical medicine course, learning combat trauma techniques imperative when dealing with firearm injuries. The firefighters have attended the local fire college, perfecting their forcible entry techniques to assist with evacuating the children. And let's not forget the chiefs, who have attended MCI (mass casualty incident) training, prepared and practised multi-company drills and drafted well-thought-out preplans. This is enhanced by strong financial backing by their administration, providing the necessary support to fund a well-trained department.

Scenario Two: The responding deputies have done the bare minimum throughout their career. They have fired the six required rounds per year to qualify at the static shooting range. They have gradually gained weight and become deconditioned, having never taken any sort of unarmed combat class or tactical weapons training. The paramedics on scene have not continued training and have become "cookbook medics", relying on their protocol books to direct their every move. Physically, the medics have also become deconditioned and the stress of the incident alone has left them exhausted.

The firefighters have not undergone any training other than that mandated by their department. They struggle to find the correct tools on their truck and go into a state of panic as the enormity of the situation hits them. The first chief on scene realises that his department has not prepared for this incident despite several near misses in the past. The agencies have allowed egos to sever relationships, preventing interagency training. Because of a lack of drills and preplanning, the units on scene begin to freelance and communication breaks down. The gunman is allowed to continue his rampage, taking more lives. Other children perish as they slowly bleed to death waiting for help that fails to make it in time.

These are obviously two extremes, but in real incidents there is most likely going to be a mixture. The rescuer going in to save your child may have trained diligently for this moment or alternatively may be nothing but a liability. Every day we have the opportunity to join one of those two groups. If you make training part of your daily routine, eat well, exercise and educate yourself, then you will rise to the challenge if, God forbid, this tragedy occurs in your city. Bury your head in the sand and have the "it will never happen here" mentality and blood may be on your hands. Literally. If we swear an oath to protect our community, with that oath goes a huge responsibility. We also swear an unspoken oath when we become a parent, and that too carries an immense duty to act.

Such tragic events are invariably followed by exchanges of blame, children's lives used as pawns in political campaigns. This nauseating behaviour by those masquerading as leaders does not protect the kids, women and men who are at risk today. I hope that an increased sense of community will begin to lessen these incidents but in the meantime, we, the sheepdogs, need to be ready. If thirty years of training results in saving one life, then all of the blood, sweat and tears was worth it. Don't just mindlessly hang your gear in the rig or throw on your vest. Make a promise to yourself and those you serve that you will end each shift a better firefighter, police officer or medic than when you started. Do that every day and, when you are most needed, you will be ready to rise up and fulfil the very promise you made when they pinned that badge on your chest.

There is a second part to this story. Three months later, I was working in our front garden, pulling weeds with my wife. The songbirds filled the air with their music and landscapers' engines droned in the distance. The tranquillity was harshly interrupted by the growing crescendo of approaching sirens. I recognised the familiar sound of ambulances, police cars and fire engines as they all raced down a nearby road, hidden by the neighbourhood's white privacy fence. The speed of these vehicles also struck a chord as this was clearly not a routine response. My heart sank as I realised the only target hazard in that direction was our teenage son's high school.

My phone vibrated in my pocket, indicating a message. "Front office is getting shot." The first text from Ethan illuminated my phone, words no parent ever wants to see. "Don't call me. We're hiding." It is a nauseating feeling to be the able protector at work yet so helpless as a parent. Living over an hour from my station, Ethan was at the mercy of other local responders. The texts kept coming, detailing shots heard and the perceived imminent arrival of an attacker. Another text. "Am in library in dark." The image of a child hiding in a blacked-out room, not knowing if he was going to live or die, filled me with both fear and rage. It was hard to believe that everything was probably going to be fine, when Florida had just witnessed the Parkland High School massacre only a few weeks prior.

Becky sobbed uncontrollably as the picture unfolded in her mind. My attempts at consoling her seemed futile as we had seen so many attacks in recent years. The feeling of helplessness was crushing. I had trained my whole career to save lives and yet I was powerless to protect my son. As with the incident at Tai's school, we frantically searched the internet for any semblance of information. After what seemed like hours, but was probably only minutes, news started flooding social media. There was a confirmed attack, but in Forest High School, on the east side of Ocala. It appeared that the incident at our son's school was a false alarm, triggered by the Forest shooting. Becky fell to her knees, relief sweeping over her as she wept. It was incredible news, but our hearts were still broken for the families who were affected.

We let Ethan know that he was safe and commended him for his bravery and composure. I later learned that Tai had spent over an hour in the dark, hiding under a desk, in the elementary school where we had shared the Code Red only weeks before. This time I wasn't there. He had joined the rest of the school, not knowing if the last thing they would ever see was a gunman entering their classroom. As the day unfolded, the kids were shuttled from the schools on buses back to the safety of their parents' arms. I think the boys still have bruised ribs from how hard we hugged them that afternoon.

As it turned out, Forest High School benefited from a combination of luck and preparation. The attacker had fired a shotgun through a classroom door, striking a student in the ankle. For some reason, he then dropped his weapon, which he had smuggled into the school in a guitar case. A teacher calmly talked to the shooter, de-escalating the situation. The school resource officer entered the school and arrested the perpetrator. His body cam showed he had both courage and composure, securing the suspect and questioning him about secondary threats. As one of the worst days in our sleepy town drew to a close, tragedy was averted because of the response of our local agencies. One young man suffered physical wounds and an entire city of schoolchildren, teachers and parents were subjected to emotional trauma.

As with previous mass murders involving guns, the mainstream media began their polarising arguments, each suggesting a different political issue as the cause of these horrendous attacks. Keyboard warriors argued valiantly from the safety of their basements. As with so many problems in the world, the middle ground was lost among the white noise of clickbait and extremism. Should each school have armed resource officers? Should each teacher be armed? Bullet proof glass? Metal detectors? Ban all firearms?

School murderers are usually not special operations soldiers but deeply disturbed individuals with little to no weapons training. The deterrent of an in-school resource officer is an invaluable preventative measure. Unlike the proposition of armed teachers, law enforcement officers should be receiving regular high-level weapons training and being kept up to date on defensive tactics. That is their job. Sadly, that does not always happen, and some of these mass murders have brought to light cases of ill-trained or unprepared officers assigned to protect our children. Any first responder agency that lowers its hiring and training bar is putting lives at stake. Our schools should not be a dumping ground for officers looking for an easy gig before retirement. A school shooting would challenge the most hardened veteran and the position needs to be resourced as such.

I've had the honour of interviewing some of the greatest thinkers on violence psychology. They never put the emphasis on one sole cause. There are many layers to this type of violence, factors that result in a perfect storm of psychosis. There is little dispute that there is often a history of both childhood trauma and mental illness with many of the attackers. Some think that certain psychiatric medication may have contributed to the psychosis. Hearing the laundry list of side effects of these drugs in their commercials means this influence certainly can't be discounted.

In his book *Assassination Generation*, Lt Col. Dave Grossman argues that violent video games are a strong contributing factor, a hypothesis that was initially ridiculed by many. Upon closer review, this philosophy makes a lot of sense to me. We are seeing the addictive elements in many gamers, playing hour upon hour, throughout the night. Once again, sleep deprivation becomes an underlying factor. In most children, this would result in nothing more than lethargy and an occasional teenage meltdown. Take a child who is already battling mental health issues and introduce sleep deprivation and you have the potential for psychosis. In the military, sleep is deliberately withheld during special operations training to find mental weaknesses in candidates. Soldiers often report hallucinations after several days without sleep. The same practice is used in interrogation techniques to break a person down.

Many children who struggle socially are drawn to these video games, yearning for the status and community they are unable to find in the real world. The military and law enforcement use similar first-person shooter programmes in their training. There have been numerous cases where murderers were incredibly accurate in their attacks, yet they had next to no actual weapons training. The video games literally desensitise emotional reactions, rewarding players with every virtual cop or prostitute they murder. Trends have shown some school shooters literally looking to outscore their predecessors, claiming their place on the death toll leaderboard.

Onscreen violence is another area that needs to be addressed. Have we ever asked ourselves as a society why slasher flicks are so popular? Many of us finish a busy work week and choose to unwind in front of a horror film, entertained by a cabin full of college kids being tortured and mutilated. Violence certainly has a place in storytelling but there is a tragic consequence of glorification. We live in a country where John Rambo can murder a hundred Viet Cong on cable television with no censorship. The same channel will blur out a woman's breast because it's deemed too offensive for the audience.

As a society, are we also contributing to the lone wolf mentality? The way modern life has unfolded has challenged the good sense of tribalism, of being part of a meaningful group. We can have a million friends on social media and yet not one meaningful relationship. We pile humans on top of each other in city highrises and sprawling suburban towns, yet loneliness seems to be rife. The pundits fight tooth and nail over gun ownership and legislation, and in the meantime these attacks keep happening. There are two areas that every one of us can control: increasing the sense of community in our immediate environment and training for an incident if it occurs. This is a multipronged response that involves us all. As parents, we can either be part of the problem or part of the solution.

A year after the Forest High School shooting, I watched an incredibly powerful presentation on the Parkland massacre by Coral Springs Fire Department. A time-coded animation portrayed the killer's movements, coupled with the live dispatch recording and CCTV footage. Heartbreaking scene photographs peppered the video, a macabre flashback to this devastating day in South Florida. Colour-coded icons represented the murderer, children and teachers. As the black dot navigated the hallways, the surrounding dots turned yellow if the person was shot and injured. A gasp filled the room every time a dot turned purple; another life lost in this senseless attack. Hardened first responder veterans wiped the tears from their eyes as the presentation concluded.

As I had witnessed at my son's school, an event like this leaves our children and teachers virtually powerless. These predators feed on fear, knowing that they will encounter little to no resistance. This is not an issue that can be addressed with pro- or anti-gun rallies. The University of Texas tower massacre occurred in 1966 and the frequency and magnitude of these murders have grown exponentially since. Is this yet another symptom of the mental health crisis that is being lost in the conversation? Guns kill people in the hands of the psychotic. Guns do not kill people when locked securely in a safe. As with addiction, these tragedies are huge warning signs of a systemic problem that we must address.

We have the responsibility to make our schools safe again. Since the introduction of fire alarms, sprinkler systems and fire drills, the last US school fire that claimed multiple lives was in 1954. America recognised the importance of prevention and those actions have saved countless lives since. We need to apply the same philosophy to the factors contributing to school violence. Mental and physical wellbeing should be at the top of our nation's agenda. These notorious killers invariably exhibited warning signs of mental illness and bullying. We can change these factors if we place more attention on the health of and compassion for our children. I hope one day we can return to a world where Code Red has no meaning.

Chapter Seven

They tried to bury us. They didn't know that we were seeds.
– Mexican proverb

It came in like any other fender bender. A one-car collision on the off ramp of a local freeway, a "truck response". As we began the journey to the incident, the dispatcher fed us more information. The engine was already on scene and had called us for extrication. I had a vantage point from the "dog house", the seat on top of the tiller truck from where I steered the back wheels. "Let's fend off here," Pete said through my headset. Pete was a salty veteran, working overtime as our engineer. I turned the wheel, sending the rear of the truck into the hard shoulder. This angle created a wedge to protect the scene from other vehicles. Emergency lights draw distracted drivers like moths to a flame, claiming multiple responders' lives each year.

   A blue sedan sat motionless on the hard shoulder, folded like a mangled metal boomerang. Tyre tracks told of the panicked path the vehicle had taken as the driver lost control on the freeway exit. Sliding sideways, the car had slammed into a steel cell phone tower before coming to rest. Inanimate objects can be unforgiving to those in motion. Fluids bled from the motionless car, running down the gentle slope of the concrete ramp, weaving through the scattered debris. The passenger side had taken a huge hit, with massive intrusion into the passenger compartment. The front door was peeled open, barely hanging from one hinge.

Gravel and glass crunched underfoot as we walked over to the vehicle. A middle-aged man lay sideways across the front passenger seat, body twisted, spine clearly decimated from the impact. His eyes were open, a look of shock on his blood-drained face, as if his last thought was stamped there permanently. Blood soaked his white shirt, trickling from his mouth and nose. The seat belt was looped over his limp body, loose from the pretensioners firing, no help in such a high-velocity side impact.

The front airbag was still behind its casing, threatening to deploy, also useless when hit from the side. The engine crew had cut the battery cables to reduce the chance of a fire or accidental airbag trigger. The back seat of the vehicle was full to the roof with plastic bags and cardboard boxes. A cream woollen blanket covered something in the back seat, but I thought nothing of it as people often had clutter in the back of their cars. A woman, rail thin and gaunt, sat on the kerbstone as the medics evaluated her. A highway patrol officer walked the skid marks with a measuring wheel, taking notes as he painted a virtual picture of the tragic scene.

The engine captain that day was Brian, a gentle giant, with a barrel chest and, usually, a warm smile on his face. Today, though, he had a different demeanour and I had a sense of foreboding that I didn't usually feel, even on the more tragic calls. As he approached, I could see the pain in his eyes. "The mom's doing okay," he said. "Mum?" I thought. I hadn't seen any children as we approached the scene. "The boyfriend and daughter were DOA," he added with visible sadness. "She's in the back." What I had thought was a pile of clothes in the back seat was actually a three-year-old girl. I walked to the rear passenger side door and pulled it open, revealing the truth previously obstructed by the twisted steel.

The blanket I had noticed earlier covered the tiny figure, silhouetting a body that was clearly missing its head. Tiny legs hung from below the blanket, too short to cover her whole body, with red sneakers over blue-and-white striped socks. There was no blood visible from this angle and every fibre in my being wanted to lift the cover and see her smiling and unharmed. Tragically, I knew that this couldn't be further from the truth. The edge of her toddler car seat protruded from the side of the blanket, plastic cup holder for her drink or snacks visible under the woollen tassels.

As I stood there, my mind would not stop questioning whether she would have been as unscathed as her mother if she had been sitting on the other side. At the time, my son was two and had an identical car seat in the same position in the back of my Nissan Sentra. A wave of devastating sorrow washed over me, and I shook my head repeatedly at the unfairness of it all. Once again, we were unable to save this little soul. We are the fixers, the rescuers, yet there was no saving this helpless little girl. A lifetime of friendships, romances, careers and motherhood snatched from her in a moment of carelessness. Life can be so cruel.

As this was now a body recovery, we were sent back to the station until the coroner was ready for us to remove the body. The food we had left sitting on the dinner table was stone cold. We reheated our meals and sat down. The firehouse kitchen is usually a hive of banter and laughter but that day's mood was dampened. The camaraderie found around the table is usually both jovial and healing, but some calls shake a crew to their core. Sometimes you can find a glimpse of humour in a tragic call, a coping mechanism, a dark outlet for the tragedy witnessed.

There was only awkward conversation this time though, as the table of mothers and fathers envisioned their own children in that car. As I ate, I made a silent promise to move Tai's car seat to the middle the moment I got home.

The tones went off for us to return to the scene and remove the little girl's body. The front passenger seat had been driven back by the impact, trapping her beneath it. Rich and I were walking to the truck when Terry ordered us to stay at the station. We both told him that we were fine and had no problem carrying out the extrication, which was true. He replied, "You're a new father. You're going to see enough images to fill your album in your career. There's no sense in adding this one." Despite the hit to my pride, I knew he was right. There are no medals for "seen the most trauma". Both Terry and Pete were close to retiring and they knew this would be one of the last times they would ever have to cut a dead child out of a vehicle. As young firefighters, we still had twenty-plus years of images to collect, victims the same age as our children as they grew up.

This one incident didn't drop me to my knees, but it has stayed with all of us to this day. It became just one of hundreds of deaths in my fourteen-year career. Some met a violent and tragic end, while some passed away peacefully in their sleep. Some died right in front of me while we fought tooth and nail to save them; others had been dead for days before we found what was left of them. Some codes went well, hitting every benchmark at exactly the right time. Some, however, were a futile attempt to save a body that was unsaveable. None of them made it. I have never saved a single person from a full cardiac arrest. The futility of doing everything you are trained to do but being unable to save a life is one of the worst feelings a first responder can have. A carcinogenic cocktail of shame and guilt.

These calls have become a part of me. It is not a "disorder", just as I did not have a back disorder when I tore three ligaments lifting a patient. That was the result of years of physical wear and tear, resulting in an unforeseen but catastrophic back injury. This also happens in the mind, both physiologically and emotionally. Each of these calls is an injury to the psyche. To a compassionate human being who chose to serve others, each tragic incident, be it death, injury or loss of a family's most cherished memories in a fire, leaves physical and emotional scars. Seeing complete strangers' lives torn apart by a lapse of concentration or murderous intent chips away at the childhood innocence we were all born with.

It reminds me of Michael Clarke Duncan's character John Coffey in *The Green Mile*. In this powerful story, he is in prison for a crime he did not commit. Despite this injustice, he continues to do good, taking the pain and suffering from people he meets and carrying it himself. Each person he saves takes a little more from his own health. One day, the burden becomes too big to carry on his own. In his speech to Tom Hanks' character, the warden, he says he is tired, not just physically but of people being ugly to each other and of all the pain in the world. He describes it as "like pieces of glass in my head". I think this is the perfect analogy for a public servant. We volunteer to be there on people's worst days, day in, day out, hoping to save a life or be the compassionate soul who holds them up after they've lost their loved one.

It's time to redefine the mental burden of the tragic events that first responders and similar professions witness on a daily basis. PTSD has acquired a negative stigma, an image of mental abnormality, viewed as some sort of weakness. This couldn't be further from the truth, but this image is so embedded that it needs to be redefined. This is not a disorder, disease, tumour or stenosis. This is the load that the firefighter, police officer, paramedic, medical examiner, ER nurse and all associated professions carry from the pain they see. To ignore or negate this is a recipe for tragedy, the catastrophic failure of the mind where the only escape is death.

Post-traumatic stress can occur after any of these incidents, and they'll accumulate, the way a retiree carries visible scars from a lifetime of physical trauma. From childhood scrapes to adolescent streetfights, the body tells a story and the mind is no different. The tragedy we witness creates trauma in the depths of our minds. The dark side, the shadow self, is an ever-present part of each and every one of us. How this manifests depends on multiple factors. The first one is something most people overlook. How much trauma do we bring into a job on day one? I look back at my childhood with so much gratitude as it was relatively non-traumatic. The worst parts of my upbringing were certainly being in a house fire with my grandfather and my parents' divorce, but they were brief moments of sadness among an otherwise charmed youth.

One of the most alarming things I have discovered on this incredible journey I'm on is just how many children experienced nightmarish trauma within their families. From being abused as a child to losing one or both parents, so many factors can wound the soul well before entering a uniformed profession. Many abused men and women actually seek out the first responder and military careers, subconsciously wanting to protect the vulnerable from what they themselves endured. I am not saying that this is a reason not to join one of these professions; quite the opposite in fact. Serving others is an incredibly healing path, as long as that past trauma has been addressed. If, however, that is not the case, it can add a significant load to the shoulders of a burdened rescuer.

To become a firefighter involves enduring a battery of

polygraphs and psychological tests, yet neglect to address any psychological needs. What if we took the money spent on these tests and instead used it for counselling sessions for new recruits? This would not only create a relationship with a mental health professional that would follow them through their career, but also give them an opportunity to address prior trauma. Rather than merely fulfil checklists and cover your ass as an employer, what if you invested in your people and gave them the tools to foster resilience? Including several counselling sessions in the orientation would be as beneficial as the physical training. Elite athletes have mindset coaches and this would be a great opportunity to maximise the performance of these tactical athletes.

The second part of this equation is basic arithmetic. As time goes on, the images stack up like some precarious game of Jenga. The longer your career, the more baggage you accumulate. Recent work-related suicides have involved veterans of their respective professions, with decades on the job. It's accepted that those involved in acute tragedies like 9/11, the London bombings and the Las Vegas shootings have a high likelihood of experiencing mental trauma. What is often not considered is the sum total of more "ordinary" calls, the accumulation of years dealing with tragedy. Most responders don't attend high-profile events so can be written off as having no justifiable reason to struggle mentally. The reality is that each shift chips a little off the psyche, like Andy's rock hammer in *The Shawshank Redemption*. The daily toll may not be felt at the time, yet the sum total can create a gaping hole.

The third element is what is going on outside of work. Life events can have a magnifying effect on an already crushing burden. Relationship problems, financial strains, family health issues and bereavements can be the final proverbial straw. Family can be your greatest support structure or your greatest source of stress, depending on its dynamic. I saw this first hand during my divorce. A single father, juggling two jobs and paramedic school while running fifty-six-hour weeks on one of the busiest rescues in the county. I was literally running on fumes, chronically sleep deprived and emotionally bankrupt. My family would comment that I looked like I was dying as they witnessed the slow unravelling over Skype calls. I was exhausted both mentally and physically.

This is where removing the stigma from PTSD comes in. Having that support from family and peers is crucial to lessening the burden. We must create an environment where we are comfortable talking to each other about the calls and how we are coping. Talking about the incidents and their effects on us is one way of offloading some of the accumulated stress. Lip service is often given to the concept of brotherhood and sisterhood. This is only a facade if we don't live up to what it means to truly be there for each other. Creating an environment where we feel comfortable talking about our stresses and worries is essential for solving the mental health crisis. This extends far beyond the firehouse to businesses and homes.

Another area that parallels this is organisational stress. This under-recognised factor is often a huge contributor to psychological illness. First responders sign on the line because they want to make a difference in the world. They train diligently and pay thousands out of pocket to follow their dream. Many then enter a department that pales into insignificance when it comes to this ownership. The department I was happiest at held us to an incredibly high standard. We trained hard, exercised together, cooked and cleaned together, with each generation taking time to mentor the next. Conversely, the one I was least happy at was resistant to any training, blocked all fitness initiatives and had chief officers with no experience as actual firefighters. This created an incredibly toxic environment that magnified the stress.

A few weeks before I was hired in Hialeah, one of the firefighters was struck by a vehicle when out on a call. He had been guiding the truck out of an apartment complex, walking behind it as a safety precaution. A speeding vehicle swerved and struck him, leaving him fighting for his life. The day before the accident, he had been telling his crew that he needed to put a new roof on his home as it was starting to leak. Unbeknown to him, as he lay in the hospital bed recovering from his massive injuries, men and women from his department reroofed his house. When he finally returned home, he wept at the sight of the shiny new metal roof as his brothers and sisters stood and cheered.

Conversely, in another department, one of my fellow classmates passed away. I had volunteered for the funeral detail and we drove two hours to be there for his family. The American flag flew proudly between the two ladder trucks, honouring his service. We waited for the last person to leave, then packed the flag and stowed the giant ladders. We grabbed some food then headed back to the station. My lieutenant's phone rang and I could see he was upset. It turned out that he had been ordered to apologise to the stations for taking too long at the funeral. Yes, the crews had complained that they had to run extra calls while we buried our brother firefighter. When I returned to my station, this was confirmed by the whining I was greeted with. Blinded by a mixture of grief and disgust, I packed my bags and went home before I did something I would regret. That was the moment I knew I had to leave that department for my own mental health.

The workplace can be a truly nurturing environment, a family that you can lean on when life throws its curveballs at you. Sadly, some workplaces can also be the main source of stress, undoubtedly a large contributing factor behind some suicides. Many people want to excel in their careers but are suppressed by managers or officers with fragile egos. Autonomy is a powerful element of the human experience. When we feel we have no control over our lives, it can be destructive. Leadership gurus around the globe agree that training and trust are the keys to creating a cohesive team. Micromanagement displays both a lack of confidence and a heightened sense of self-importance. Creating a positive, challenging and nurturing workspace is vital for the psychological wellness of a department or company. This is what investing in people really means.

This leaves the fourth and most important element in this perfect storm. The coping mechanisms that we choose are the only part of this equation that we can truly control. A healthy outlet for post-traumatic stress can help unload some of this burden. The most common positive outlets are exercise, family, faith, nature and altruism. Healthy body, healthy mind is not just some catchy phrase. It is true both physiologically and psychologically. Exercise releases endorphins and flushes out cortisol, resulting in reduced stress levels and an increased sense of wellbeing. Having a functioning body eliminates additional stressors such as pain and ill health. Having enough sleep also helps achieve wellness and hormonal balance. This takes a concerted effort from the first responder who works shifts.

Post-traumatic stress becomes a "disorder" when we stop controlling our shadow and it begins to control us. Choosing poor coping mechanisms further breaks down the pillars that were holding us up. Drugs, alcohol, infidelity, gambling and other self-destructive practices weaken our defences in an already compromised structure.

Three years ago, I was at a theme park with my wife. It was an incredibly hot day under the scorching Orlando sun. As we walked to one of the rides, a woman passed me pushing a stroller. Because of the heat, she had placed a cream blanket over the top to shelter her child. Tiny legs protruded from the cover wearing bright red sneakers. A wave of adrenaline rushed over me as I immediately flashed back to the fatal wreck I'd run on ten years prior. I told my wife that I needed a moment and sat on a concrete bench, processing what had just happened. That kind of flashback haunts some of our professional men and women. It was short lived and some controlled breathing brought my heightened response back to normal, but I can't imagine suffering from that repeatedly.

So let's remove the disorder from this acronym and start acknowledging that we are all exposed to traumatic stress. Create a positive environment that enables healthy conversation around the dinner table, a chance for all of us to say how we feel. Help lift those who are hurting and learn from those who have pulled themselves out of the darkness. No first responder is spared from post-traumatic stress. I hope we can remove the stigma once and for all and stop any more of our brothers and sisters from feeling they have nowhere to turn. Remember, if you bury the seeds, they will keep growing in the dark until they can't be contained any more.

Chapter Eight

My body could stand the crutches but my mind couldn't stand the sideline.

– MICHAEL JORDAN

THE BAR WAS HEAVY, two hundred and twenty-five pounds to be exact. The knurled grip tore against my skin, shoulders fighting to stay in position as gravity resisted the lift. Legs pushed against the earth as my hips drove forward to full extension, weight held against my thighs. I dropped the barbell, then fell flat to the floor, immediately springing back up, clapping my hands above my head. The cloud of chalk added an overtly dramatic puff into the humid air. "One!" the judge shouted. Nine more reps of a deadlift then burpees were still ahead of me. The crowd cheered as seven other firefighters performed the same movements, lined up alongside me at the 343 Hero Challenge.

The event had been created by three Orange County firefighters, Ric Segrest, Dave Coughlin and Tom "Bull" Hill, to honour the 343 FDNY firefighters lost on 9/11. The competition was also a fundraiser, choosing a different charity to support each year. First responders and civilians came from all over Florida to participate in this gruelling event. Pictures from the New York attacks adorned the walls, positioned to inspire exhausted participants to dig a little deeper. Each heat began with a recording of that tragic day's dispatches, with crews sent into the World Trade Center never to return to quarters. Additionally, there was a skill station to honour Carl Andriano, a young firefighter Orange County lost to cancer.

I pulled the last rep off the ground, dropping to complete the tenth burpee before moving to the next exercise. I paused for a moment, summoning the strength for the next movement. "Remember who's on your back, Geering!" my judge shouted at me, challenging the exhaustion evident on my face. He was referring to the six names written on the skin of my back, each one of them a local first responder who had died that year. Little did I know that, five short years later, twenty-eight names would join them, written from shoulders to hips. Thirty-four men and women who were murdered on duty or died from work-related physical and mental health issues. My lungs burned, the thick humidity resisting each laboured breath. My body was drenched with sweat, a feeble physiological attempt at drawing heat from my red-hot skin, seemingly ineffective as it puddled below me. I looked up and saw Steven Ranravenswaay, an Orange County squad firefighter who had just been diagnosed with cancer. He stood on the sidelines, mask on, cheering us on. Two years later "Shakey", as he was known, would join the names on my back.

The final event was a medley of firefighter movements. Heavy sandbags were held as we squatted and thrust them overhead. Kettlebells were swung, large diameter hoses pulled, rolled and carried. The final obstacle was an extremely heavy victim drag, simulated with firehose laden with multiple weights. One by one, we leaned into the load, painstakingly slowly. The crowd roared, drawing the dregs of energy from deep within us. I inched across the finish line, collapsing on the floor in exhaustion. The cheering continued as the last participant fought to move the incredible burden. I stood up and walked over to him, joining the crowd that had already formed. He listened to their advice, changed his grip and pulled with all his might. The immense weight began to move, and as he got faster, the crowd got louder, exploding in applause as he crossed the line.

Some will say that brotherhood and sisterhood are dead but I disagree. An event like this will renew your belief in such a philosophy. I have watched men and women go to a dark place to complete this competition. Their motivation is to honour their ailing and fallen brothers and sisters and there is no greater incentive. Those struck with work-related disease, fighting for their lives, being encouraged by the support. The families of those we lost seeing that their loved one is not forgotten. This event makes me so proud to be a firefighter and stand shoulder to shoulder with some of the greatest humans on planet earth. Although there were prizes for making the podium, the reward was seeing the community band together, unified for a powerful cause.

There is another reason I tell this story. Just five months prior I had a near career-ending back injury. I never wanted to get hurt on the job but I'd always envisioned that, if I did, it would happen in some heroic way. I saw myself showing off scars to a wide-eyed audience while I recalled how I had just extricated the last preschooler when the car shifted or building flashed. The reality was that my career was almost ended by a 160-pound panic-attack patient who was sure he was dying. As consummate professionals, we had offered to take him to the hospital for further evaluation, which he accepted. The rescue vehicles we had in that department did not dump or lower, so the deck was ridiculously high. As I went to load the patient into the back, the stretcher caught on the edge. I went up on my toes and arched my back to gain the extra couple of inches needed to push the stretcher into its cradle.

When people say they heard a pop, they are not exaggerating. It felt like I had been stabbed in the back by an invisible assassin, leaving no visible mark, just searing pain. In thirty-nine years I had never had even a twinge, no less an injury. I slowly climbed into the front seat and drove to the hospital while my partner tended to the man in the back. Every bump and turn felt like a fire being stoked in my lumbar spine. Sciatic pain was searing down my left leg, as if acid were pouring through my veins. It took all of my strength to assist my partner in removing the stretcher at the hospital and completing the transport. After the patient was offloaded onto the emergency room bed, I told my fellow medic that I was hurt and contacted the chief.

The appropriate steps were taken to begin the worker's comp process and I was told to report to the local urgent care clinic. After an x-ray and physical exam, I was offered a smorgasbord of pharmaceuticals, from opiate painkillers to steroidal anti-inflammatories and muscle relaxers. Knowing that this was a traumatic injury, I tried to get the ball rolling on physical therapy but was told to report back to the clinic in three days. Upon my return, I was greeted by a different PA, a morbidly obese man who appeared exhausted from the short walk from his examination room. He informed me that he would not authorise physical therapy and ordered me to take the meds. Yes, you heard me correctly. I was ordered to take drugs by a physician's assistant at the clinic used by all the local first responder agencies. Needless to say, I don't do well being told what to do by a medical professional who can't even take care of his own health, so I sought out the original doctor and finally got my referral for an MRI and PT.

Trauma to the human body is equivalent to damage to a car from an accident. The injury has to be addressed and the structure rebuilt and strengthened. I don't know too many drivers who would be happy with a fresh coat of paint over a smashed-up vehicle. The human body is no different. Prescribing medication as a long-term fix to trauma is, in most cases, both ineffective and, in my opinion, a violation of the Hippocratic Oath. "First do no harm" resonates deeply with me as a paramedic. I have a set of protocols that dictate my medical choices for my patients. If I deviate from these, I put the patient at risk of potential harm or even death. So why doesn't a firefighter or police officer get this same courtesy extended to them when they are hurt? Denying physical therapy and other movement practices condemns the patient to a lifetime of chronic pain.

I began the journey to heal myself without the chemicals that had been sold as my only solution. I attended my initial orthopaedic visit with a local doctor I both knew and trusted. I was told the initial diagnosis was a type II tear to three of the ligaments connecting my L4, L5 and L6 lumbar vertebrae. This caused significant herniation of the discs and severe pain. When I lay on my stomach and raised my leg, one of my vertebra would actually rotate. The physical pain was evident but I underestimated the mental cost of a serious injury. I can't describe what it is like to not be able to pick up your child. I am a very hands-on father and, at five years old, my son loved to be picked up and flung around the room. Unlike a broken wrist or sprained ankle, back pain affects everything you do. It hurts to sit, to bend, to stand, to twist and even lie down. I couldn't kick a ball, run, swim, do martial arts, a CrossFit workout or even make love to my wife. Every type of movement was agony and it took its toll physically, mentally and emotionally.

The temptation to take the pills they had offered me was overwhelming. Beer became an easy way of numbing the pain and helping me get to sleep, but then I just felt even worse in the morning. The irony is that pain stops you getting the very element that you need to heal: sleep. To add to this, I had been taken from the profession that I loved. The ability to make a difference in someone else's life was gone, which just added to my feeling of inadequacy. One day I was riding an engine, cinching up the straps of my SCBA on the way to a structure fire, the next I was struggling to get out of bed. I could feel myself slipping into some sort of depression, feeling emasculated by this inability to move the way my body was designed to. As first responders, we pride ourselves on our ability to rescue and protect. There is a primal feeling of vulnerability when injured. To quote author Arthur Golden, "A wounded tiger is a dangerous beast." This sudden plummet down Maslow's hierarchy of needs jars the soul. The sudden inability to protect your wife and children is crushing.

I got pissed off, really bloody pissed off. Firstly, at myself for allowing whatever anatomical weakness caused this. Secondly, for the awful lack of treatment options offered to a man who uses his body to put food on his family's table and to protect his community. This injury was legitimately threatening the two loves of my life: my family and my career. I decided to devote every day to not only healing but getting fitter and stronger than ever before. I went to physical therapy four times a week, spending an hour and a half per session. My fellow patients were elderly as Ocala has a large retirement community. The physical therapist was not used to training occupational athletes so I had to help steer them in exercise choice. The most basic of movements had become agony and it took going to a dark place to find the strength to push myself through the therapy.

The treatment would end with a ten-minute ice compress, where I would sit and contemplate how next time I would push even harder. I would also try to figure out what went wrong. I had worked out four times a week, practised yoga from a Rodney Yee

DVD at least twice a week, ate well and also took time off when I felt my body needed it. Why did I suddenly break lifting a relatively small patient and not on the hundreds of emergency scenes that required high levels of physical exertion? How had I got hurt when on paper I did everything right? I was woefully unaware of the damage both sleep deprivation and sitting can inflict on the muscular system.

I found a chiropractor and paid out of pocket for treatment four times a week as worker's comp wouldn't cover it. His initial assessment confirmed the damage in my back but also showed how I had developed an excessive curve in my spine. The sessions began with an adjustment, followed by thirty minutes of traction and exercises to begin to reverse the damage. His philosophy made a lot of sense. There's no point getting adjusted if you haven't addressed the muscle imbalances that caused the subluxation in the first place. If muscles are adding undue stress to a joint, they will simply pull the bones back out of alignment. What made this chiropractic philosophy so effective was the understanding that lengthening and strengthening was needed alongside correction.

Traction involved sitting in a chair and stretching the neck with a weight hung from the forehead. This addressed the shortening of the muscles in the front of the body that pull the head and shoulders forward, a common posture in today's technological world. Each chair had a television in front, which would play informative videos. One day, sitting there with my head pulled back, I watched a man lead a series of exercises that looked similar to yoga. He stated that this was a movement practice that would strengthen the back and thus fix back pain. I asked my chiropractor about the video and he told me how he had had great success with it personally. He instructed me to follow it every day before our appointment.

My progress had been painfully slow up to this point. My

back would start to feel a little better and I would begin to get encouraged. The next morning, I would wake up, praying that the pain was gone, only to be greeted by the same agony. Getting out of bed was an effort in itself, and putting on my shoes was damn near comical. I started to incorporate the video into my morning routine and was amazed that my back actually felt better after it. The video was "Twelve minutes of Foundation Training". Foundation Training is a back health routine developed by chiropractor Dr Eric Goodman. He too had become so frustrated by the lack of options for his own back injury that he developed this movement practice. After a week, the progress was so good that I started doing it as part of my physical therapy and showed my therapist this incredible system. My back got stronger and stronger and the pain less each morning. With the reduction of pain, my sleep improved, magnifying my recovery.

The effects on physical therapy were astounding. Exercises that had me looking like my geriatric counterparts were now easy again. I started to recreate the movements that I would need to be able to do on the fireground. Thick rubber bands simulated advancing a hose or pulling a ceiling. I carried a weight-laden bucket up and down a step ladder. A huge mistake is to return to duty before the body is completely healed. In one of my sports medicine classes, the professor explained that an injury can feel 100 per cent healed when it reaches around 80 per cent. That is why so many injuries reoccur. It is imperative to ensure that you give your body ample time before returning to work. My philosophy was to train as if the very first call back was a structure fire because it very well could be. I've never seen anyone given a medal for coming back from an injury too soon, yet so many of us feel compelled to do so.

In addition to the therapy, I had been back in the gym as soon as I was able to. I scaled movements using a PVC pipe as a baseline and began increasing the weight as my body got stronger. I replaced the pipe with a training barbell, then a regular one, adding weight incrementally. I used weighted sleds to replicate dragging a victim and advancing a hose line. Kettlebells simulated the heavy equipment we are required to carry. Sandbags were another incredible tool to strengthen the posterior chain, mirroring the dead weight of an unconscious patient. After three and a half months, I had strengthened my back to the point where the pain was not only gone but I could complete the tasks required of a fully functional firefighter.

Three months later, I was deadlifting 225 pounds for reps at the 343 Hero Challenge. This wasn't a superficial removal of pain; this was a legitimate fix to an injury that could have forced me to retire from the profession that I know I was born to do. I managed to convince my administration to send me to California and I became certified in Foundation Training. Upon my return, I gave the class to every single firefighter in my department, giving them the tools to avoid the terrible journey I had been on. So many of us don't begin this road of self-discovery until we ourselves get hurt. In an ideal world, we should work on our strength and mobility while we are young to prevent these injuries ever happening. Sadly, though, pain is the best teacher.

Coupled with noting the lack of recovery, I had learned that this injury came from muscle imbalance placing the joints in biomechanically horrendous positions. Years of sitting, one of the side effects of modern society, had taken its toll on my body. My pelvis was tilted, my hamstrings and glutes were short and weak, my shoulders were rolled forward and my neck was craned over my chest. We forget how much time we sit in the fire service. Driving to and from calls, typing reports, eating meals and watching hours of online training videos. People say sitting is the new smoking and I agree. After six months of my recovery routine, my posture had shifted completely and I was pain free. I could squat properly, deadlift with good form and, most importantly, do anything a five-year-old asked me to do. To this day, the journey has not stopped. The anatomical damage will always be there, like a scar, so I have to work constantly on my body like the tactical athlete I am.

I sought out Julien Pineau of StrongFit to further improve my movement patterns, especially carrying the heavy loads a firefighter is required to. He found more imbalances and helped me further strengthen what was weak. The strongman movements replicate so many fireground tasks. The equipment we use is incredibly heavy and we often need to carry it significant distances. The CrossFit movements were fantastic for conditioning but they often lacked the element of moving weight over distance. By adding overhead yoke carries, sled rope pulls and other posterior chain exercises, both my mobility and strength improved. A single injury or muscle imbalance can start a cascade of damage to the human body. It takes time and patience to reverse-engineer the problem and also address the root cause.

I can honestly say that I move better as a forty-six-year-old man who got beat up in firefighting, stunts and the martial arts than my twenty-one-year-old former self. The medical professionals I initially saw created a path to failure. Without the exercises I used, my back would never have healed and the pain would always be with me. The drugs they prescribed could have been the "first one is free" slippery slope to opiate addiction. In the fourteen years of my career, only a small percentage of the overdose deaths I ran on were from illegal street drugs. The majority of these tragedies, which tore the hearts out of families, were from pills prescribed by a physician, legally under our current "healthcare" system. I'm not blaming all doctors but I am underlining the fact that the current system is not working and something needs to change. I know firefighters who are addicts and others who died from this affliction.

As first responders, we need to understand that many injuries are treatable without medication or surgery. This is a bitter pill to swallow as it requires patience and hard work. The body is amazing but it needs time to heal. We have to look at ourselves as athletes because we are. Tactical athletes. Athletes have a team around them as peak performance does indeed take a village. Nutritionists, trainers, chiropractors, psychologists, coaches and more. If you can't physically find these people then begin to educate yourself and become your own advocate. Question everything you have been taught up to this point and start looking at how it affects you personally. If your doctor is morbidly obese, maybe they are not the best source of wellness advice. If your personal trainer has no idea of the physical demands of a first responder, maybe find a coach who does.

William Osler, physician and co-founder of Johns Hopkins Hospital, once said, "One of the first duties of the physician is to educate the masses not to take medicine." Medicine certainly has its place and the emergency drugs I use at work can be extremely effective. Medicine for chronic illness and injury, however, can result in a lifetime dependency on chemicals. In the realm of painkillers, this can lead to the destruction of both health and family. It's time we started challenging this system. When you get hurt, research how you can heal the trauma holistically. You'll be amazed how many injuries can be treated without pharmaceuticals or traumatic surgery, getting bones glued or screwed together, ensuring a lifetime of immobility and arthritis. You are your own advocate and the more you understand about your own body and the treatments available, the more power you have over your own health.

I was able to stand side by side with men and women from my profession and honour the fallen just five months after my injury. My son watched as I dug deep to resist the inner quitter. He had seen me when I was first hurt, my frustration and pain through rehab, the inability to play with him. But then he saw the growth, the recovery, becoming more and more active with him. Now he stood in the muggy steel building, cheering his dad along, his the only voice I truly heard. He saw with his own eyes that an injury is not an automatic disability but merely a hurdle. I hope that philosophy stays with him. Our children need to be educated in the power of functional medicine, which looks at a person through a preventative and holistic lens. The human body is an incredible creation capable of powerful innate healing. It just needs time, nutrition, movement and sleep. These principles are not complicated, but they don't make companies wealthy. They will, however, help forge a healthier nation, both physically and mentally.

Chapter Nine

Too much sugar leads to a heavy body and too many distractions lead to a heavy mind.

– Naval Ravikant

THE MAN WAILED, BODY shaking with each sob as he rocked back and forth on the kerb. He held his head, fingers digging into his blond hair, as if clawing at the horrors that unfolded in his mind. His eyes were closed tightly, refusing to see more. He fell silent for a moment, then looked up at the red minivan that lay on its roof in the middle of the road, a macabre vessel amid a sea of broken glass. There was a beat, and reality hit him. "No, no, no!" he screamed, as the truth forced itself inside his guarded mind, projecting the images once more. We caught each other's eye for a moment as I hurriedly carried the extrication tools to the side of the vehicle. He howled at the sight of the "jaws of life", sending him into a higher wave of torment.

The van was eerily still, a stark contrast to the devastating impact that it had endured moments earlier. Jagged metal pushed deep into the space where a mother and child sat, a concave imprint of another vehicle stamped into the frame. A woman's slender arm hung limply from beneath the white side impact airbags, as if draped by a mortician. A stuffed panda lay in a puddle of coolant and petrol, button eyes staring as if traumatised from what it had just witnessed. The emergency lights illuminated its reflection in the fluid, apparent horror magnified with every strobe. What had happened in the moment before the impact? I thought of my son, sleeping peacefully after a day at the beach, clutching his sock monkey without a care in the world. Was this child sleeping, dreaming, before the collision tore her favourite toy from her hands? I shook the thought from my mind, focusing on the task at hand.

Heather, our paramedic, snaked her way into the vehicle through the shattered rear window. She cut the seatbelt that was choking the little girl, hanging like a marionette in the upturned van, and she slowly lowered her to the ground. The mother hung lifelessly from her seat, blood dripping off her hair, pooling on the tan headliner below. Heather covered the child with a blanket, protecting her from both the debris and the grisly scene surrounding her.

"I'm Heather. What's your name?"

"Lucy," the child replied between sobs.

"My friends are going to get you out, okay Lucy? You might hear some loud pops and bangs but that's normal, okay?" Heather was trying to reassure her. "I'm right here with you."

"Help my mommy!" Lucy cried. "Help her!"

Heather paused momentarily as she processed the white lie she had to tell the child to keep her calm. "We're going to get her out too," she said with a warm smile.

The girl's screams pierced the sound of our hydraulic tools as we fought to gain entry to the back seat. Metal jaws bit deeply and methodically into the folded steel, slowly creating a purchase point to attack the latch. Powerful spreaders stretched and sheared the sheet metal, steadily widening the gap to the terrified child inside. The power unit's engines roared as they shifted gear, amplifying the pressure needed to overcome the van's integrity. The choking smell of petrol and glass dust filled the air, burning our throats. Our engineer aimed a charged hoseline in our direction, ready for any sudden ignition of the gases that would engulf us all in a ball of fire. Our progress seemed painfully slow, as if time itself was holding its breath.

The door finally gave in, an explosion of energy as it jumped out of the sliding rail. Two more cuts and it was out, giving Heather and Lucy access. They placed a hard collar under her chin, protecting her potentially injured neck. The KED, a rigid jacket used to stabilise the spine, was wrapped around her and buckled tightly. She continued to cry, this time for her father as she sat immobilised, surrounded by complete strangers dressed in strange clothes. I assumed her dad was the man I had passed, and was relieved one parent had survived. Heather had done an amazing job of calming Lucy, compliant despite the trauma of being cinched into a contraption that limited her movement. She answered the questions as Heather continued her trauma and medical assessment, an encouraging sign. In unison, we lifted her out of the upturned van and onto the stretcher.

"Daddy!" Lucy screamed as her eyes caught the sight of three of our engine paramedics performing CPR on another man. He had been ejected from the vehicle and had landed twenty feet away in the long grass next to the highway. My heart sank, realising that I was wrong about her father. The crew were obscured by the vehicle, blocking my view of the male victim. "Daddy, Daddy, Daddy!" Lucy cried as she witnessed the medic cutting into her father's throat, desperately trying to secure an airway with a cricothyroidotomy. The man's face had suffered horrific trauma, devastated from the impact with the windshield. Inserting a tube directly into his trachea was the only option left, having exhausted every other way of saving the man. We lay Lucy flat on the stretcher, buckled her in and helped load her into the back of the ambulance. We closed the doors and the rescue drove off, sirens wailing as it headed to the paediatric trauma centre.

"Time of death 10:34 pm" I heard a voice relay to dispatch through my radio. The medic working on the father had "called it". A traumatic full arrest means an almost zero chance of recovery and, despite the crew's efforts, Lucy's father died on scene. They pulled the yellow sheet over his lifeless and bloodied body and started gathering their equipment. The second extrication team had managed to gain access to Lucy's mother, who was also confirmed deceased. We regrouped, taking a few minutes to decompress before beginning the long process of cleaning tools and sterilising medical equipment. Emotions were mixed. On the one hand, we'd managed to save a little girl, yet tragically she'd lost both her parents. My heart physically hurt at the thought of her hearing the news. Her entire life had been changed forever, innocence snatched in the blink of an eye.

A highway patrol trooper walked over, wearing the same sad look that adorned our faces.

"Any idea what happened?" I asked him.

"Witnesses reported seeing an SUV driving aggressively, snaking through traffic. They stated that the driver lost control and slammed into the minivan, sending it rolling off the road. A bypasser tried to get to the family inside but couldn't get the doors open. Apparently, the mother was screaming her daughter's name over and over, before finally falling silent. Just awful."

"Where's the driver now?" I asked.

"There, the man on the kerb," he said, pointing to the sobbing figure as he was handcuffed by another trooper.

In my career I've lost count of the number of people I've

encountered wailing with tears of self-pity, crying to their god after putting the importance of an appointment, drink or text reply before the lives of a family they had just snuffed out. What's heartbreaking is that all of these accidents were preventable. All of them! I've never responded to a true "act of God" event like the San Francisco earthquake or the tsunami in Thailand. The lives I've seen snatched in fourteen years as a firefighter were all due to selfish acts of human arrogance. An impatient driver whose sudden lane change pushed a motorcyclist under the back wheels of a semi truck. A drunk driver who blew through a stop sign, instantly killing an elderly woman who had the right of way. A self-absorbed motorist who cut through a petrol station to avoid a red light, killing an eight-year-old girl innocently riding her bike on the pavement. The list goes on.

Early in my career, these deaths were more likely to be alcohol related, but the distraction of smartphones is becoming the primary underlying cause of vehicular homicide. That an Instagram post or text emoji would be more important than a human life seems unthinkable, but that's exactly what's happening. A pity party is not going to bring back the lives they took. We have found ourselves far from being the selfless men and women of the World War II era, who fought for the lives of complete strangers in faraway countries. The roads are filled with drivers who believe they are the centre of the universe, and it's killing our men, women and children in genocidal numbers. Globally, we lose roughly one and a half million people each year to traffic accidents alone.

I was incredibly fortunate to grow up on a farm in England with rolling fields to practise on and an abundance of motorised vehicles to test my skills. I spent my youth tearing up and down the hills on a rusty yellow front loader dump truck. It was a crank start, requiring me to turn a handle to fire up the diesel engine, much like the original cars. It had to be gripped a certain way to avoid losing your thumbs when it roared into action, taking the handle spinning with it. For years, driving was essential for the farm tasks I helped with after school. Mucking out stables and spreading the manure under trees and taking hay to the horses in the furthest acreage.

Safety was always drilled into us as farms can be incredibly dangerous, especially for children. Every summer, my dad, who was a veterinary surgeon, used to make us watch *Apaches*. This gruesome public service announcement portrayed a group of English kids playing on a farm. One by one, they died a horrible death of their own doing, drowning in a slurry pit, falling into machinery and crashing a tractor to name a few. British PSAs are known to be gut-wrenching, but this one excelled. Watching a child slowly die after accidentally drinking rat poison was traumatising for any seven-year-old boy. That said, it did engrain in me the severity of those actions. A long list of names, real children who had died on farms, preceded the end credits.

In the UK, the driving test is something to be revered. The average person takes around three attempts to pass. The written test is not usually the challenge. The driving portion, however, is the true crucible. Drivers must pass tests of multiple skills near flawlessly, from parallel parking and reversing around a corner to navigating roundabouts, hill starts and much more. With very few automatic vehicles on the British roads, these manoeuvres are usually tested in a manual transmission vehicle. I had a huge advantage being a farm boy and had progressed to driving the Citroen C15 veterinary van on the road. I still took several months of driving lessons with a professional instructor before finally feeling ready for the test. I passed first time only because of the immense amount of practice I was able to accrue. Additionally, I took several more classes after, to ensure competence on the motorway. Learner drivers are not permitted on them until they pass the test, so this was another daunting new skill I had to learn.

After moving to the US, I had to test for a Florida driver's licence. Feeling like a seventeen-year-old all over again, I nervously performed the pre-checks. Once my mirrors were set and our seatbelts were buckled, the driving examiner told me to start off down the road. For the next ten minutes we drove around a couple of residential streets and then manoeuvred in and out of a parking space. He then told me to return to the driving centre. I thought that it must have been a warm-up for what was yet to come. "Congratulations! You passed," he said with a big smile. Although I was amazed and relieved, this incredibly low bar didn't really sink in until I became a firefighter and got to witness the ripple effect personally. Most kids in the US pass their driving test on first attempt and with very little preparation. There's no focus on the why behind much of the safety elements of driving or the true consequences of one moment of poor judgement.

When training standards are lowered, there is usually a direct correlation with an increase in the number of injuries or deaths. This is true in the fire service as well as on the roads. I have personally witnessed both sides of this and the consequences of the lower test bar are terrifying. At one end of the training spectrum, I worked for a department whose hiring standards were extremely high. Orientation was three weeks of drilling truck company operations, engine evolutions and emergency medicine skills. This was followed by a gruelling year of probation with tests every four months. The probie attrition rate was twenty-five per cent, holding the line on the standards they stood by. The result was a motivated, highly trained team of firefighters who protected, among other things, one of the famous theme parks on the west coast.

Conversely, on the east coast, another department had minimal hiring standards and orientation consisted of only three weeks of "show and tell". The administration had historically wanted the responders out of view from their theme park guests. This had included being told to drag cardiac arrest patients backstage before they could even begin CPR. I personally ran a code while the staff conducted business as usual around us. The firefighters' union had even prevented training in the heat and rain and blocked all fitness initiatives. Near misses were ignored, swept under the carpet with no lessons learned to grow from. As with driving, this low bar is a recipe for disaster, inviting a scathing after-action report on a tragic death toll.

When you look at the statistics, the United States has four times the road traffic fatalities per capita than the United Kingdom. With both being similar cultures, the only measurable variable is the level of training. Merely teaching the workings of a car does not reinforce the motor skills of driving. Memorising rules of the road does not foster understanding of why such rules are in place. A disregard for true understanding of the why behind the speed limits, safety precautions and signalling has destroyed lives all over the planet. Teenagers have the highest likelihood of killing themselves or others in a car accident. This is counterintuitive when you think that they should be the most cautious and well trained, before poor habits can set in.

What is lost in this threadbare testing system is the kindness element that is essential to safely navigating steel deathtraps around the country. For example, using the indicators (blinkers in the US) lets those around you know your intentions. Based on the lack of use by many drivers, the one pound of pressure needed to flick the signal is clearly exhausting. By not signalling, you're proclaiming your self-importance to the world, keeping your next manoeuvre a close secret for other drivers to figure out at the last moment. Keeping your distance from the vehicle in front vastly decreases the likelihood of an accident. It also changes the relationship on the road from selfishness to consideration for other drivers. In 2008, four people were killed on I-75 when seventy vehicles collided in heavy smoke and fog in Ocala. The worse the conditions, the more caution and consideration are required.

The biggest problem is that people drive assuming that nothing bad is going to happen. The reality is that we should all adopt the opposite philosophy. Items fall off trucks causing drivers to break suddenly or swerve. Children run out into the road, transfixed by a ball they were chasing. Medical emergencies or sleep deprivation cause drivers to cross lanes into the path of oncoming traffic. Understanding the responsibility of being a driver is paramount to the safety of other road users. Driving aggressively because you left the house late for work risks the lives of every other man, woman and child around you. No appointment, date or job is worth killing people over. Again, kindness and compassion trump selfishness every time.

When we embrace this attitude, driving is not only safer but also more enjoyable. So many fatal wrecks are caused by angry drivers navigating around other bad drivers. When you share the road rather than fight over it, it flows, ultimately getting everyone to their destination faster and in one piece. If driving standards are held high or made higher, we will address one side of the problem that's needlessly killing the innocent. If each of us takes responsibility for the potential danger and drives with compassion, then it's a two-pronged attack on the devastation that we see on the world's roads. Phone use, drinking or drug use and driving aggressively or selfishly kill and there's no bringing back the lives you stole. You can be part of the solution. Don't be the person on the kerb.

Chapter Ten

*The opposite of addiction is not sobriety,
it's human connection.*

– JOHANN HARI

"I'M GOING TO GIVE it one more chance. If it doesn't work, that's it!" I stood there, stunned, my mind searching for an appropriate response as he downed another Bud Light and crushed the can, lobbing it into the overflowing rubbish bin. I knew exactly what Sam was referring to. After several failed attempts to get sober, he had reached a breaking point. Two separate times he'd checked himself into an inpatient addiction facility and twice he'd returned, straight back into the dark place he'd tried to escape from. The mixture of frustration and surrender was evident on his face as he paced around his kitchen.

I had met Sam at my gym about a year prior. He was a firefighter too, so we would partner up and do a Hero WOD, a workout of the day to honour fallen warriors. I would fight to keep up with his furious pace, a futile attempt, especially if there was heavy weight involved. He was known to do "Murph" every Sunday, in full bunker gear, masked up and breathing air. Sam had been given the nickname "Cyborg" by his fellow firefighters, as he never seemed to fatigue and remained stone-faced throughout. He taught at our local fire college and I took several special operations classes under his instruction. The admiration his peers and students had for him was obvious, a true leader who led from the front. He had also passed the prestigious Smoke Diver training, the highest-level physical test in the fire service, which he then helped run.

But things slowly started to change. His near-superhuman performance began to dwindle, with workouts often leaving him visibly fatigued. His seemingly unending endurance was replaced with intolerance for intensity. The poker face he was so famous for was gone, exhaustion and pain now clearly visible on his face. Sam started to miss training sessions, not something that rings alarm bells as the fire service has a way of forcing additional shifts, so it's not unusual. It was only when he was AWOL for coaching sessions that we finally started to realise that something could be wrong. The reason many addicts fall between the cracks is that the change is slow, gradual, like adding hot water to a tepid bath. It's only when something catastrophic happens that people finally realise how many warning signs they missed. The giant red flag hit me when Sam failed to show up for yet another coaching session and our gym owner expressed genuine concern for his welfare. As I look back, I remember posting a picture on social media of a group of us after a gruelling workout. Someone commented, "That guy looks like he's seen some shit!" He meant Sam. I was about to learn just how tragically correct that comment was.

Realising the seriousness of this downward spiral I drove straight to his house, praying that he had not become another statistic in the suicide epidemic. His truck was parked outside, confirming my suspicions that he hadn't left his home that day. Repeated doorbell rings elicited no response from inside. I started knocking, louder and louder, rattling the aluminium door in its casing. Eventually a voice from inside shouted wearily, "Gimme a minute!" A figure approached, silhouetted in the frosted glass of the door's window. The handle slowly turned and the door opened a third of the way. An acrid stench of cheap beer and vomit wafted out into the evening air, catching me momentarily off guard. Sam's eyes were bloodshot and his skin pale as the white door frame that barely held him up. I knew this was not the time for a deep and meaningful conversation so I let him know that we were worried about him and that I would be back to check on him the next day. And that's when I ended up listening to my friend plan to take his own life if this final attempt at treatment didn't work.

Sam was a veteran, not only of the fire service, but of the military as well. He had served his country for well over a decade, as a leader for much of it. Now he stood in front of me, his once laser-focused eyes now mottled red and drained. It's a strange dichotomy watching a man so physically strong but with eyes betraying the true pain he's enduring. A stranger seeing this scene might immediately jump to a shallow conclusion that he was a drunk. This judgemental kneejerk has killed so many in crisis, shamed into silence.

Sam had been repeatedly sexually abused as a young boy and carried that immense secret into adolescence. As a teenager, he found the numbing effect of beer allowed him to push the trauma deep into the back of his mind. Liquor was a crutch through adulthood until he made the decision to join the military. The Marines had been the positive structure he was missing in his life. As a natural athlete, he thrived in bootcamp, self-confidence growing with each challenge he conquered. He discovered belonging as he was forced to work as part of a team, forging a deep sense of tribalism that had been missing for years.

Alcohol was not accessible and the physical training gave him the positive release his body had been craving. The void he'd been filling with booze was replaced with the camaraderie of his unit and the positive outlets of exercise and purpose.

Sam had a goal to join the Marines elite as a recon sniper. His exemplary performance in bootcamp had opened the door for selection. Excelling both academically and physically, he was accepted to the Marine Special Operations School. Once again, he rose to the challenge, and with each new level the pain was pushed deeper and deeper from his consciousness. At the end of 2000, Sam graduated and was assigned to a Marine Raider regiment in North Carolina.

With this new position came a new level of freedom. The grinding drill grounds and early morning wake-ups were replaced with evenings out with the men from his unit. Bootcamp had kept his mind busy, a welcome distraction from the past. Now, however, he had time to reflect and the trauma came rushing back like a maelstrom in his mind. The magnitude of his addiction took hold and within weeks he was drinking himself into oblivion again. The alcohol immediately affected his performance and, two short months later, he was given an ultimatum: fall back into another regular Marine unit or separate from the military altogether. He chose the latter, not knowing that eight months later two towers would fall in New York and he would have seen the combat he trained so hard for. That regret would become yet another chink in his armour.

Civilian life was like a punch to the gut after the brotherhood he'd experienced in the Marine Corps. Sam found work in construction and would follow a day in the Florida heat with a night of drinking alone in his apartment. One day he was chatting to a friend who worked as a part-time carpenter around his full-time firefighting shifts. As he told fire service war stories, Sam realised that this was the career he had been searching for. He had, as many alcoholics report, a moment of clarity. Sam stopped drinking cold turkey and began the journey through EMT and fire school. He landed a job in one of the most respected departments in the state and immersed himself in the profession. For years he signed up for every technical class and conference he could attend. Rising through the ranks, Sam became an authority in the training department and an integral member of the special operations team. He took all of the overtime that was available, unaware that the job was an unconscious distraction from the trauma he'd experienced twenty years prior.

After ten years of sleepless twenty-four-hour shifts mitigating people's tragedies, cracks began to develop. The newness of the profession he loved so much had lost its allure. What was once an exciting fire became a routine event that barely raised his heart rate. The learning curve lessened as the calls began to seem repetitive. The void that he'd managed to fill with the excitement and adrenaline of the fire service life began to open up again. A nasty divorce added another layer of stress, compounding his mounting personal and professional trauma. Exhausted and heartbroken, Sam picked up his first drink in a decade. As had happened in the Marines, the ripple effect of addiction bled into his career. Unlike in many departments, however, Sam's chief recognised the underlying problems and fought his corner while he sought help. Two failed attempts later, here he stood gloves up for his final round.

A widely accepted analogy in the mental health realm is the concept of a bucket overflowing with traumatic events. I had used this term for several years until I realised it just doesn't fit where addiction is used to fill the void that trauma has left behind. Reverse the concept, however, and you have a hypothesis that works perfectly. Imagine the body and mind craving a full bucket to function. In a healthy child, the bucket swells with the fruits of good food, play, parental love and deep sleep. A little water spills out after a grazed knee or parental scolding for momentary selfishness, but it is soon refilled when laughing at the family dog chasing its tail in the kitchen.

Now imagine the forty-year-old firefighter. For each trauma, there's a hole in the wall of the bucket. For some, like Sam, the first hole may have been huge, from his childhood molestation, haemorrhaging the essential fluid needed to feel whole. This alone is enough to drain the mental health of an individual if not addressed. Now add many other traumas. His parents' divorce, a hole. Isolation through the addiction, a hole. The loss of a dream career, another hole. Sleep deprivation, ten years of seeing tragedy, his own divorce; more holes, leaving the bucket looking more like a colander.

As the number and size of the holes increase, the need to refill what's lost grows. The body yearns to replace the emptiness with something, anything, just to feel whole again. Alcohol, opiates, gambling, social media, extramarital affairs, porn or any other form of escapism all momentarily replace the loss. The volume is temporarily filled but the holes continue to leak the contents, an exhausting battle in both body and mind. The bucket is now technically full yet the contents are not bringing happiness as the vessel knows it is broken. More holes begin to appear as the effects of addiction magnify the problem. Alcohol and drug use further rob the body of rest and recovery. Finances are strained, struggling to afford the drugs or gambling used as a crutch. Broken relationships perforate the bucket further until some reach a point of no return.

Conversely, positive coping mechanisms have a twofold effect in the right direction. Exercise, mindfulness, counselling, nutrition, community, altruism and the healing effects of nature slowly reduce the damage. As the holes narrow, the effort to retain the contents becomes less of a struggle. The smaller the holes get, the easier it is to fill the bucket with nurturing contents. The feeling of health and vitality dissuades the individual from choosing the "quick fix feel goods" that drive most addictions, investing instead in further repairing the damage. The bucket will never be completely sealed, requiring maintenance work as we navigate this beautiful and traumatic journey we call life.

Sam's drug of choice was both legal and socially acceptable. We drink to celebrate and we drink to commiserate, at weddings, funerals and sporting events, with very little stigma attached. There are many who find themselves addicted to controlled substances to fill their voids. They are forced into the shadows in many countries of the world. I remember watching the reality show *Cops*. Foot pursuits and car chases, ending with the perpetrator bloodied up and in handcuffs as the officers searched them and their vehicle. More often than not, the "criminal" had a small amount of weed or crack for personal use. Not a dealer or a smuggler but an addict. This is a perfect illustration of how far we have strayed when it comes to how we look at addiction.

The prohibition of illicit drugs began in the 1930s based solely on the racist rantings of men like Harry Anslinger and William Randolph Hurst. Prior to this time, many of these drugs had been used medicinally. After alcohol prohibition failed, Anslinger had to justify his role and began the journey to criminalising drug addiction. He was once quoted as saying, "There are 100,000 total marijuana smokers in the US, and most are Negroes, Hispanics, Filipinos, and entertainers. Their Satanic music, jazz and swing, results from marijuana use. This marijuana causes white women to seek sexual relations with Negroes, entertainers, and others." This story is told in detail in Johann Hari's incredible book *Chasing the Scream*.

Alcohol prohibition had been a disaster, originally created as a result of pressure from extremist Christian groups behind the American Temperance movement. Contrary to such beliefs, crime skyrocketed after prohibition took effect. Organised crime thrived, with notorious figures like Al Capone profiteering from illegal alcohol sales. Americans still drank, but they were forced to use the unregulated and often dangerous black market. The law was repealed in 1933, dismissed as a complete disaster. There are no turf wars between beer and whisky companies today, no speakeasies raided by the police. Alcohol is undoubtedly still an incredibly unhealthy coping mechanism for mental ill health but its use and treatment are socially accepted.

Drug prohibition reached far outside the US borders as Anslinger started to pressure other world leaders, and it ultimately became the norm in the UK, Australia and many other nations. This so-called war on drugs has cost the American people over one trillion dollars since 1971. The US prison population has risen from 350,000 in 1970 to over 2.3 million today. We lose one person from opioid overdose every sixteen minutes, part of the 70,000 overdose deaths in America each year.

To compound this issue, mental health practitioners have found incredible success combining counselling with psychotropics like MDMA and psilocybin. The psychological barriers that trauma creates are greatly reduced, allowing patients to truly address the issues they had locked away. Organisations like MAPS (Multidisciplinary Association for Psychedelic Studies) are leading the charge in this area. This treatment has yielded incredible results, especially for PTSD. The prohibition of useful pyschotropics has created unhelpful barriers in the use of this powerful treatment. This just adds to the death toll of drug prohibition, with suicides and overdoses amplifying the body count.

As a paramedic, I witnessed this crisis first hand on a weekly basis. Searching for a jugular vein in the neck of a heroin addict because their arms were so scarred from repeated injections. A firefighter whose wife found him dead in his bed after an accidental heroin overdose. The innumerable murders as gangs fought over turf so they could peddle drugs to the addicts in their community. I lost count of how many teenagers I covered with a yellow sheet as their families shrieked and wailed in the background. These children died caught up in a war, pawns in an international drug ring. As with Capone, prohibition had given power to the underworld. Today American teens die on the streets as the kingpins sit in their mansions, counting their bloodstained money.

As longitudinal studies go, the research on drug prohibition reveals it as one of the most epic failures of human intervention. The planet is inhabited by millions of people with mental illnesses manifesting as addiction. They are driven to the dark corners of society to score drugs of unknown origin and unpredictable strength. They cower from the police, knowing that being caught will result in a criminal record, yet another barrier to the dwindling hope of recovery. An arrest history all but eliminates any chance of a rewarding career and drastically increases the chances of poverty and homelessness. Despite their illegality, drugs find their way into prisons, used to exert power and as tools for predatory actions, further feeding the addiction.

A few years ago, my mother had mentioned in passing that Portugal, where she had emigrated twenty years prior, had decriminalised all drug use. In the late 1990s, Portugal had the highest addiction rate in all of Europe. The traditional prohibition methods simply weren't working so a group of politicians and doctors decided to try an innovative approach. They proposed changing the laws so addicts were seen as medical patients instead of criminals. This certainly did not pertain to drug dealers or smugglers, who would still be dealt with harshly. Two years ago, I had the honour of talking with Dr João Goulão, the man who spearheaded this initiative. As I sat in his Lisbon office, he recounted the success of his country's drug decriminalisation.

In less than ten years, Portugal had dropped from the highest addiction rate in Europe to the lowest. Now, if an addict is detained, they are brought in for an interview and educated on the addiction and the psychological treatment that is available to them. Although this is not mandatory, once the fear of arrest is removed, the addicts are able to come out of the shadows and seek help. They are funnelled into programmes that prepare them to rejoin society. Incentives are given to employers to hire recovering addicts, further bolstering their self-worth.

Safe injection sites have been set up where drugs can be taken under the watchful eyes of medical personnel, virtually eliminating accidental overdoses. As with most economics, demand affects supply and illegal drug sales and smuggling have plummeted. Police officers are safer on the streets and can now focus their efforts on the serious crimes. Courts have been dramatically freed up and of course incarcerations for drug offences all but eliminated, taking the strain off the prison system.

Another incredible man I had the pleasure of interviewing is Tom Eberhardt, governor of Norway's Bastøy Prison. Nestled on an island off Oslo, Bastøy is heralded as one of the most humane and successful prisons on earth. Norway has one of the lowest recidivism rates in the world at a meagre 20 per cent, a stark contrast to the 76.6 per cent of American prisoners who reoffend in the first five years after release. The focus in Norway is true rehabilitation, with prisoners living in actual houses. They cook, clean, maintain jobs and pursue education. The philosophy is to prepare them for life back in society because most prisoners are released one day. The result is that Norway's prison population per capita is only 10 per cent of that in the US. By contrast, as with the war on drugs, the Philadelphia prison model used in the US, UK and other countries, based on the belief that solitary confinement forges penitence and encourages reformation, has proven to be woefully ineffective.

Having spent a career personally witnessing the failure of both mental health and addiction policies, I feel it's certainly time we tried a different approach. These are not addicts. They are men and women who were once giggling toddlers without a care in the world. Then life happened. Some saw trauma as children, others in combat overseas or on the streets of the communities they protect. Where some were able to find support in a healthy direction, others fell into the trap of addiction. This didn't make them any less human; rather, they are humans in greater need of support and compassion from their community. Many of the religious doctrines teach us about kindness and compassion, yet many of our laws kick squarely against them.

We were once called to an infamous street in Orlando. A young woman was found dead in a dumpster, discarded like human rubbish. There was almost disdain by some of the responders when it was discovered she was a known addict and prostitute. They were wrong. She was a human being, someone's daughter, a beautiful baby girl who probably brought immense joy to her parents before whatever set of misfortunes led her to this blue steel coffin. A young woman with dreams of travelling the world, of being treated like the women she saw in movies, maybe of having children of her own. Now she lay lifeless, surrounded by empty cardboard boxes and rupturing bags of waste. Her last moment one of pure terror, strangled under the blinking neon lights of the neighbouring strip club. That is the ugly face of drug prohibition.

Sam made an incredible recovery. Three was a charm in his case and the rehabilitation centre provided him with the tools he needed to finally overcome his addiction. He told me that a counsellor had helped him see that he was the victim of a predator, to give himself permission to stop blaming himself. The guilt and shame that had embedded themselves into him, like emotional vines strangling joy, were exposed and discredited. He was able to look beyond the mistaken belief that PTSD is some kind of weakness, that everyone else is doing fine. This notion is one of the biggest myths among the military, first responders and civilians.

We are all fallible, each of us struggling to overcome the cards we have been dealt. Some cope well and owe it to those who are struggling to become a beacon of hope.

Sam returned to full duty and is preparing for promotion to chief level. He has been sober for two years and now heads up a wellness initiative that brings recovering addicts together, using exercise as an outlet and a community. After returning to his position, many of the colleagues he worked alongside began confiding in him about their own addictions. The stigma around this had kept them silent, and some had also contemplated their own deaths. Sam's turbulent battle almost killed him. His courage saved not only his own life but undoubtedly many others too.

The suicide crisis has found some recognition in today's society, but addiction has yet to free itself from the stigma. We can't address the mental health epidemic without including all forms of addiction. Globally, we lose almost a million people a year to suicide, alcohol kills two and a half million and tobacco claims over five million lives. These are all products used to dampen emotional responses. People argue tooth and nail over the gun issues yet children continue to die in our schools. Nothing is clear cut, however. If you address an issue from both sides simultaneously, success is far more probable.

We truly can change the world, but it is going to take kindness and compassion all the way up the chain. The people who live on the streets are not "bums"; they are human beings. The notion that they dreamt of being homeless one day, yearning to beg for change and live under a freeway bridge, is ridiculous. Many of them are our veterans who fought for their country, only to be abandoned upon their return. Just because some of us were able to navigate life's pitfalls doesn't mean that we should belittle or dehumanise those who didn't. As Michael Watson once said, "Strong people don't put others down, they lift them up."

We are in a compassion and kindness crisis and the answer is painfully simple. Look to the countries that are having success in these areas. Portugal's and Switzerland's drug policies, Norway's prison system, Finland's education system and the UK's National Health Service. Their success is largely down to the fact that human growth and wellness are at the core of their philosophies. There is absolutely no reason why we can't have the humility to learn from each other, comparing notes to create the best versions of our countries. I thank God that Sam was able to find the light in his darkness. He had friends, fellow firefighters and the right facilities to create an environment for success. We owe it to every other addict to make the light easier to find.

Chapter Eleven

I will apply dietetic measures for the benefit of the sick according to my ability and judgment;
I will keep them from harm and injustice.

– The Hippocratic Oath

Royal Victoria Park is nestled in the northwest corner of Bath, a beautiful Roman city surrounded by the rolling hills of the English countryside. This adventure playground is the closest thing most children growing up in rural Somerset would ever get to Disney World. Adorned with wooden structures, swings, ropes and even a crude zipline, it was a wonderland for childlike fantasy. Parents would bring their munchkins and set them free, hoping they would exhaust even a fraction of the infinite energy young children seem to have. I would spend hours running around, enacting stories as an SAS soldier, climbing over the monkey bars and flying down the zipline like Action Man, my favourite toy.

Despite the complexity of some of the equipment, the traditional seesaw was usually one of the most popular playthings. A simple plank of wood balanced over a fulcrum allowed two riders to launch each other into the air. The most comical moments were when a mismatched couple would jump on and the lighter of the two was stuck in the air, helpless while the onlookers laughed. I was small for my age and often found myself on the wrong end of this disparity. I learned to dish out some payback by leaping off the seesaw as the other end rose, sending the offender crashing down to earth in a heap. "What's with the childhood story?" I hear you ask. Let me tell you another one, not quite so uplifting this time.

The man was motionless, hanging out of his silver SUV as if poured from the white leather passenger seat. His head and shoulders bore his immense weight, while his feet remained jammed in the foot well. His wife screamed in utter disbelief. Based on the location, this was clearly the beginning of a vacation trip for them. The tragic scene jarred against the serene beauty of the surrounding manicured resort. The patient was morbidly obese so it took several of us to pull him away from his car to an area where we could begin CPR. Lifeless eyes stared into mine, seeming to beg me to save him from his inevitable death. He was pale, ashen in fact, as if all the blood in his body had drained into some internal void.

Effective compressions were challenging as his body was riddled with both subcutaneous and visceral fat, strangulating every organ and blood vessel. IV access was near impossible, as his body had become so deconditioned that his veins were atrophied and buried deep under thick adipose layers. I fought to get an airway but his stomach had other ideas, sending up an unending flow of gastric contents, overriding his epiglottis and violating his airway. My partner searched for a landmark to drill in an IO, the "bone gun" that delivers a needle directly into the tibia. This was a challenging task in legs that were so swollen, looking ready to burst from the fluid his failing heart had been unable to move.

It's a strange feeling working a code knowing damn well the person has no chance of surviving. With an airway full of vomit and no heartbeat showing on the monitor, the chance of moving oxygenated blood around the body becomes close to zero. We continued our efforts as there is always that crazy miracle story giving a minute amount of hope. In our focused mindset, we barely noticed his wife's screaming. There's a certain flow state when running an emergent call like this. A different mode that removes emotion to enable us to perform whichever lifesaving tasks are needed at the time. It's the beautiful interaction between years of training, a high-stress environment and a calm mind. For that moment, you work as a cohesive team, needing very few words. It's after the call is over and the adrenal dump has diminished that the true magnitude of the tragedy hits you.

Our lieutenant tried to calm the woman and tease out the man's medical history in the hope that it might provide some lifesaving information. She began a seemingly endless monologue of ailments and medications, in remarkable detail, recalling drug names, doses and frequency. Our local protocols called for twenty minutes working an asystole code before "calling it" if all of the criteria were met. A common misconception is that every emergency patient needs to go to hospital. The reality is that care rendered at the roadside by paramedics is far more effective than moving them to an ambulance and driving to the hospital as this vastly reduces the ability to provide good-quality CPR.

As the last of the twenty minutes concluded, I made the decision to terminate the code, another feeling I'll never get used to. We stepped back, leaving the evidence of every intervention in place for the medical examiner. As we began to pick up our equipment, I happened to glance at the giant bag of medications the patient's wife had been describing. It suddenly dawned on me that none of them had worked. This man had thousands of dollars' worth of the latest and greatest drugs and he had died a horrible death anyway. He had used them for so long that his wife could recite the complex chemical names and the exact dose of each. On paper, the hypertensive drugs may have brought down his blood pressure, yet he had been dying all along, regardless of numerical changes.

"So what the hell does this have to do with seesaws?" I hear you cry once again. Well, it all comes down to homeostasis. The human body has an innate desire to be in balance, in a place of equilibrium as when both kids on the seesaw are suspended above the ground. When this balance is upset for a long time, the body begins to fail. The man in this story is just one of five million lives lost annually to this abandonment of the body's natural balance. The equation is painfully simple but the application seems to elude so many. Energy in versus energy out pretty much sums up the key to good health. Of course, there are nutrients that we all need, but scurvy and rickets are not our primary killers in the abundant West. That being said, there is a haunting irony in the fact that many people in developed countries are overfed yet malnourished.

There are 168 hours in a week. The most dedicated athlete will train for three or four hours a day, with the average active person training three to four hours a week. I'm no Rain Man but that leaves around 164 hours of low activity, especially by those with sedentary jobs. As much as first responders like to believe we are kicking in doors 24/7, the reality is that driving emergency vehicles and computer work takes up a large part of our shift. What this means is that one side of the seesaw is going to have a very skinny child on it. If your energy in (the refined calories you consume) far outweighs the energy used in a week, the thin kid continues to get stuck in the air. As time goes on, the systems in the body that require homeostasis to work optimally begin to develop disease. Blood vessels become inflamed and narrowed. The ability of the pancreas to produce insulin diminishes. Sex hormones become suppressed, exacerbating the global degeneration in the body.

The point I am trying to make is that, although I am a huge proponent of exercise, no matter what the Lycra-clad orange guy on QVC tells you, it is only a small, albeit important, part of overall health. What we eat truly dictates a large portion of how our body functions. I recently heard a doctor say, "Don't wait for science to prove what you already know is true." Despite the spectrum of wellness solutions, this simple concept has held true. The quality of food, however, has only recently come to the fore. If you consume more energy than you burn, it will be stored in your body as fat. As a species, we most likely were not getting three square meals a day back in primitive times. There would have been periods of feasting and times of famine. Fat storage is an inbuilt survival mechanism to avoid death in times when food is sparse.

In today's society, this biological tactic has become our own worst enemy. The digestive tract is designed to break down whole food, in the form it was plucked from the ground or tree, allowing the body to absorb the nutrients at a steady state. By contrast, processed foods are often refined to a powder, with many of the nutrients long lost in the factory processes, and where even starches are basically pure sugar. This highly milled form of carbohydrate is rapidly absorbed by the body and creates a huge insulin spike, resulting in enormous stress to the pancreas. The sheer enormity of calories consumed also overwhelms the body and forces it to convert the sugars to fat. This is then piled onto organs and under the skin in the same way that sludge builds up in and around a car's engine. This vicious circle compounds as the organ systems begin to fail.

So back to the weeping wife whose soulmate lay dead in the middle of a beautiful park, tube in his throat and a needle sticking out of his leg. The medications he had amassed were for high blood pressure, high cholesterol, cardiac arrhythmias, excess fluid, depression and more. Although each drug most likely affected the metric it claimed to address, did it actually improve health? Clearly not. Paramedics get to see behind the curtain of society. The ill health of many of the world's people is shockingly clear to us. As with every issue, this is a double-edged sword. Of course, individuals need to take ownership and take their health seriously, and I will get to that in a moment. On the other side of the equation, however, is an industry selling the false narrative that many diseases are irreversible and the only solution is a lifelong prescription of pharmaceuticals.

Drugs play a very important role in many areas of medicine. I definitely wouldn't want to undergo a knee replacement without anaesthesia. I have seen the incredible effectiveness of Narcan reversing an opiate overdose or dextrose on a hypoglycaemic diabetic. In chronic disease management, however, there is a trend of completely disregarding lifestyle changes in place of pharmaceuticals. Of course, there are some cases where drugs can be a stepping-stone towards changing habits and regaining health. What does not seem to be happening is a concerted effort to remove the drugs after health targets are met.

Another abuse of medication is to treat so-called risk factors. I've lost count of how many young, fit firefighters I know who have been prescribed medicine for high cholesterol. This is despite all other elements of their health being completely within normal limits. Recently, the rigid guidelines on cholesterol were dramatically loosened when the medical community discovered that there are several forms. The common sense view seems to be that if you have several elements of ill health, such as obesity and high blood pressure, high LDL cholesterol can increase the health risks. Conversely, a healthy individual is not going to have health issues from elevated cholesterol alone.

As important as it is to underline taking ownership by the individual, we must also acknowledge that we are setting our citizens up for failure. We allow pharmaceutical companies to bombard us with commercials claiming that a magic pill will fix all of our ailments. The stark irony stares us in the face when we hear an unending list of side effects. A depression medication that may cause sadness, depression, anxiety, suicidal thoughts and even death may not be the healthiest choice. Despite this, Americans spend over $300 billion a year on prescription medication. The juggernaut that is the drug industry doesn't make that money from altruistic practices. As the saying goes, there's no money in healthy or dead people. The industry makes a profit from keeping people sick. This is not a conspiracy theory, just basic economics.

So what is the extremely complex and complicated answer to this epidemic? Well, I hate to disappoint but the answer is really bloody simple. Eat how your great grandparents ate.

Clearly, there are some areas we have improved upon, but the fundamental message remains true. A hundred years ago, food was grown without chemicals and its DNA had not been altered, so the body still recognised it as a member of the plant family. Livestock roamed in paddocks, eating the food that they actually wanted to eat. Cows ate grass, chickens pecked at seeds and insects, and pigs foraged for acorns and roots. There were no antibiotics or hormones needed as these animals weren't crammed in industrial warehouses, being fed ground-up animals while their peers lay dead and rotting at their feet.

Winston Churchill once said, "Healthy citizens are the greatest asset any country can have." Industrialisation of our food has been the single biggest contributor to ill health in the Western world. Turning food into food-like products with no nutritional value has created an epidemic of disease in many countries, killing more people than all wars combined. This food is being fed to our children in schools, grooming them to follow the same road to shortened lifespans as the current generation of adults.

Our fruit and vegetables are poisoned with chemicals, sprayed by workers wearing level B hazmat suits. The meat is from animals so sick that they are pumped with antibiotics just to keep them alive long enough to slaughter. Milk comes from cows loaded with hormones to keep them constantly lactating, with any remaining nutrition destroyed during pasteurisation. Let's not forget the corporations genetically engineering seeds, allowing high levels of pesticide and thus affecting the health of both the consumer and the environment.

Scientific studies have shown that cancer was rare prior to the industrial revolution and that the rise in rates of the disease is likely linked to changes in diet and environmental factors. Both external and internal toxins are undoubtedly related to this disease. The cancer treatment industry is worth an estimated 160 billion dollars, so once again we have to question motives. When you research using nutrition to treat cancer, the idea is rebuked by many of the medical giants. Once again, we are taught that surgery, chemotherapy and radiation therapy are the only options for oncology patients. Insulting an already depleted immune system seems counterintuitive. There is undoubtedly power in looking at the diet of a cancer patient. Fasting is finally being recognised as a powerful adjunct to treatments. If diet is not addressed, we are missing a huge piece of the puzzle. Bolstering the body's immune system with clean food makes physiological sense, yet it is rarely the focus of treatment.

It's time that we took control of our food and therefore our family's health. Buying food from local farmers who subscribe to traditional holistic farming methods is not only cheaper but greatly reduces our carbon footprint. Mother Nature has shown us the dramatic positive changes possible after the forced isolation of the COVID-19 outbreak. Venice's canals have run clear for the first time in decades. Los Angeles, London and Wuhan have seen a huge improvement in air quality. We can make an impact on our food in the same way, demanding the naturally produced foods our ancestors enjoyed.

Why transport food thousands of miles when most can be grown in your own county? We vote with our money and if we, the people, demand quality food at the community level, we can truly change the health of our loved ones and our neighbours too. Visit your local farmer's market and buy food that has never been in a box or bag. These markets are usually cheaper than the pesticide-laden imported foods at the stores. An ounce of prevention is worth a pound of cure.

Learn to cook like our ancestors did. What was once a skill passed on from generation to generation has been lost in the convenience of fast food and television dinners. One thing that is consistent in most fire stations is crew dinners. The station will decide on a meal and shop for the ingredients between calls. By the way, contrary to urban legend, the public does not pay for this food. All meals are paid for by the firefighters themselves. The process of cooking itself creates a greater appreciation of food and is most definitely a bonding experience. Many hands make light work, so the more crew or family members you can involve in the process, the quicker it will be ready.

The smells of the kitchen prepare the body for a meal, priming the digestive system. Once the food is ready, turn off the electronics and sit around a dinner table and talk, the way firefighters have for decades. This will not only nourish the body but also the soul. Being present when you eat also slows the meal down and ultimately lessens the amount eaten. This time is also crucial for mental health, fostering the relationships that are at the core of our tribal experience.

One area rarely discussed when it comes to obesity is the psychological element. As with alcohol and opiates, food can also become a coping mechanism for those with a history of trauma. For some, the fix may be the sugar rush, the momentary dopamine hit that sweet treats and sodas provide. For others, obesity may be unconsciously deliberate, a way of dissuading sexual attention. We make the arrogant assumption that everyone wants to look good. For someone who was abused as a child, this may be the furthest thing from their mind. To them, attention may equal danger. I have watched many gym members train diligently several times a week yet still fail to lose any fat. Until we address the reasons why we turn to food for comfort, we're avoiding the root cause of the problem.

What you eat will either heal you or hurt you. You and you alone get to make that decision, and the more of us who choose health, the more available this type of food will become. We focus on terrorism while our fellow citizens are dying in genocidal numbers. It's time we started a new revolution, reclaiming our nation's health and carving a brighter future for our children. Joel Salatin once said, "If you think organic food is expensive, have you priced cancer lately?" Invest wisely!

Chapter Twelve

*I do not believe we can stop perfecting new ways of dying
until we have found new ways of living.
Every new life-way ought to prevent a new death-way.*

– Haniel Long

THE CHURCH WAS MAJESTIC. Polished organ pipes adorned the walls behind the stage, rising like dawn sunbeams towards the heavens. The light was dim, magnifying the sombre nature of the gathering. The auditorium's acoustics amplified the piano music that greeted the mourners. Sniffles and suppressed cries punched through the serenity. A white fleck would catch my eye as tissues were snatched from their packet and passed to someone weeping. The congregation was split evenly down the middle. Family and friends sat on the left side, an array of dark colours. The uniformed personnel sat on the right, a wave of deep navy Class A dress suits worn by the first responders.

Firefighters, police officers, EMTs and paramedics had travelled from all over the state as a show of solidarity. This was my community at its finest. The stage was illuminated, lectern flanked by colourful flowers arranged into a Maltese cross, the symbol of the fire service. To the left of the pulpit, a worn yellow bunker coat hung on the wooden handle of a pick-headed axe, "Andriano" stitched into the back. Bunker pants rolled over well-used black leather boots sat to the left of the jacket, with a fire helmet perched on top. The coffin was draped in patriotic red, white and blue.

The image of a young man in uniform proudly holding a brand new fire helmet shone from the projector screen. Carl Andriano was just twenty-four when he lost his battle with cancer. He had become a firefighter at the age of nineteen, assigned to one of the busiest companies in Orange County. Station Thirty had a reputation for being extremely busy and was filled with passionate and aggressive firefighters. You only bid for a firehouse like that if you had a burning desire to be right in the middle of the action. They fought a lot of fires and saw more than their fair share of tragedy in the community they served. Carl was an integral member of that cohesive crew.

For the next hour, people told stories of Carl's short yet incredible life. His crew recalled hilarious stories from some of the calls they had run together, the laughter a momentary break from the crushing grief felt by all. Carl's fiancée spoke of their romance and the man she fell in love with. I admired her incredible courage, fighting her tears, determined to tell the story of their life together. She recounted their plans for future adventures, family desires that were now snatched from her. The finality of death was so abrupt and unapologetic.

As I sat there shoulder to shoulder with hundreds of mourners, it struck me that this was the ripple effect of losing one single person. Each life that Carl and his crew had saved was one less church full of mourners. Conversely, for each person they'd lost, a room full of men, women and children wept. After losing a patient, we pack up our gear and prepare for the next call, giving little further thought to the impact the death will have. This was a sobering reminder of the magnitude of that impact experienced with every person a firefighter loses throughout their career.

As the last speaker concluded their heartbreaking goodbye, the room fell silent. Snare drums beat slowly as the haunting sound of bagpipes echoing in the adjoining hallway drew closer. The sombre music filled the church, acoustics magnifying the chorus. I flashed back to my days lifeguarding at the Hampstead Heath ponds in London. On the way to work, I'd often pass a piper, who would practise for hours on the top of Parliament Hill. I liked the sound of the bagpipes then. The music would carry off into the air like dandelion seeds. But that was a time before firefighter funerals, before parades saluting caskets draped in American flags. I truly hate the sound of bagpipes now.

The honour guard followed the pipes and drums, marching with regimental precision. Every step, head movement and salute was drilled to perfection. A drummer kept the beat as they moved around the casket, reminiscent of a disheartened German cuckoo clock. One member marched to the shining brass bell standing alone in a wooden frame. Slowly and deliberately, he rang it three times and paused, repeating the sequence two more times. The bell has been used for centuries to mourn the loss of firefighters and this tradition still holds true today. As we listened to the bell's last toll, the silence was deafening.

A female dispatcher's voice came through the church speakers, a tradition I'd heard so many times in my career. "Orange County to Firefighter Carl Andriano… Orange County to Firefighter Carl Andriano… Orange County to Firefighter Carl Andriano, last call…" After the final call, the dispatcher announced that Carl Andriano had not responded and his last call signified his passing. I have never been able to stop the tears betraying my true emotions, and this time was no different. There was no British stiff upper lip or stoic Hollywood actor's face. The room erupted in a chorus of devastating deep sorrow and I cried along with them.

The firefighter at the bell rejoined his honour guard as they collectively saluted his casket. In unison, they lifted the American flag, ceremoniously folding it into a neat triangle. One gathered Carl's helmet and they slowly marched to the weeping family in the front row. There is no more heartwrenching sight than to watch a folded flag being given to grieving loved ones. Carl's helmet was presented next, tragic memorabilia of the young man they adored. I remembered the countless children of first responders I'd watched, handed their mother's or father's helmet or duty cap, never to see it worn again by their beloved parent. A grieving child is unquestionably one of life's greatest injustices.

In the past five short years, we have lost eight firefighters that I worked alongside and many more in neighbouring departments. The causes of death weren't building collapse, backdraft, exploding grain silos or raging wildfires. Cancer killed six of my close firefighter brothers, including Carl, an aneurism took another and cardiac arrest took several more. The affliction extends to mental ill health, where accidental overdose and suicide claimed even more of my brothers and sisters. The sad thing is that this statistic seems to be viewed as the "price of doing business", which illustrates my point. Protecting your community is not a business and the men and women who sign up for this position are not expendable like some out-of-date stock in the back of a warehouse.

Computer science professor Randy Pausch once said, "If there's an elephant in the room, introduce him!" Let me say that that elephant has been in the room for a really long time and should have been paying rent for years. We have been battling factors that kill us for decades and we have a lot to thank our forebears for. Whether it's a firefighter's bunker gear and SCBAs, or deputy's ballistic vests and Tasers, advocates have fought tirelessly to keep first responders safe. Buildings are being made safer to protect the occupants from fire. Cars have been developed so well that a crew responding to a seemingly fatal wreck are often met with unscathed passengers. Leaders in their field have educated us on the dangers of carcinogens, advocating cleaning bunker gear, removing vehicle exhaust fumes from bays and aggressive post-fire decontamination.

Sadly, just like Randy Pausch, who tragically died from pancreatic cancer, diseases such as cancer still take an unacceptable number of first responders and civilians every year. Another more alarming fact is that once a first responder retires, they are no longer counted in these statistics. The mortality rate of first responders doesn't factor in any of the retirees who served for decades. The irony is that retirement age is when the chronic diseases linked with their line of work manifest. The current statistics are just the tip of the iceberg of the true cost of service to their community.

Why are so many first responders dying despite increased education about fitness, decontamination and safety? The answer is so simple it is almost comical, although there is nothing funny about the deadly results. According to the Organisation for Economic Co-operation and Development (OECD), the average American work week is 34.4 hours. The average firefighter work week ranges from 48 to 56 hours. This is the bare minimum, not factoring that many departments will continuously force their firefighters, dispatchers and police officers to stay additional shifts to cover staffing shortages. This can put the average work week well in excess of 70 hours.

Imagine for a moment if you told a candidate for an office job that they would probably be forced to work seventy-plus hours a week without sleep. I'm pretty sure you would have an empty office. Now don't misunderstand me, we have to band together when all hands are required. In the event of a hurricane, wildfire or multiple-alarm fire, there is no question that extra bodies are needed. Every department will have incidents where they will need extra staff. The problem is when this requirement becomes a weekly event. This of course parallels other professions that also work similar hours, with the medical resident or junior doctor being prime examples. The Japanese experience so many people dying from overwork they named it: Karoshi.

The shift schedule has always been sold as if it's some heavenly secret, hidden from the public. One day on, two days off sounds like an amazing pseudo-retirement arrangement. The reality is that by the time you get off shift, you have already worked an eight-hour day, rendering the "two days off" null and void. The more appropriate description is three days on, one day off. When you factor in that those eight hours are when you are supposed to be sleeping, you introduce the true elephant in the room: sleep deprivation.

Instead of well-rested first responders making life-or-death decisions, the reality is that they are worn down and running on fumes. While the person bagging your groceries or grooming your pet most likely had a good night's sleep, the driver of a twenty-five-ton ladder truck driving "lights and sirens" and opposing traffic may not have slept for several days. Green Beret, West Point psychology professor and author of *On Combat* Lt Col. Dave Grossman has stated that there is no doubt that sleep deprivation is killing first responders. Grossman has seen this in the military, law enforcement, fire service and EMS, and also cites it as one of the underlying causes of the school shootings seen around the globe.

First responders live an average of twelve years less than their civilian counterparts, often dying within five years after retirement. They are anywhere from 1.2 to 2.1 times as likely to develop various cancers. This is more disturbing when you factor in that most young recruits are some of the most physically and mentally resilient members of the population. The disruption of the circadian rhythm can cause a cascade of physiological effects from limiting testosterone production to inhibiting insulin production. If the body cannot switch to the parasympathetic state that sleep allows, it cannot repair itself.

So what is the answer? Shift patterns have been contested for decades. Twelve-hour shifts? Splits of ten and fourteen hours? Forty-eight hours on, ninety-six off? The algebraic analysis goes on. The problem is you can try to divide fifty-six hours a million different ways but at the end of the day it still adds up to fifty-six hours. I compare this to a Rubik's cube. You can spin the colours around to your heart's content yet the cube remains the same size. We are never going to fix the underlying issues that are killing our first responders and associated professionals until we address the work week. There is no denying that we need to protect our communities at night. A majority of fires and criminal activities occur outside of office hours and we need to be ready to respond. The answer to this is not to chop up the day into bite-sized pieces. The sleep medicine world has acknowledged the split shift, often used by law enforcement, as the worst shift schedule because of the continual circadian rhythm disruption.

The answer is to give our first responders, doctors and other shift workers time to recover from the hours they work. In the fire department, the twenty-four hours on, seventy-two hours off shift pattern would be the best configuration. This would mean that a firefighter would truly have two full days to recover from twenty-four hours without sleep. This also means that when they are forced to stay additional hours, there would still be some time to recover before the following shift. When you do the maths, this still adds up to a forty-two-hour week, well above the average American's schedule.

So ask yourself this. Would you want the paramedic fighting to save your child's life to be sleep deprived? Would you want the armed police officer who pulled over your teenage son to be running on fumes? Would you want the firefighter cutting your mother out of a car with power tools to be fighting to stay awake? Obviously, the answer is a resounding no! So let's start changing this profession that we love so much for the better. Let's take proactive steps to improve the service we provide, making it safer for our community.

We have the power to save lives, not just those of our profession but also the lives of those we serve. Sleep deprivation has undoubtedly contributed to many civilian deaths. Whether it was a poor decision by a police officer, a missed medication by a paramedic or a missed victim in a primary search of a house, lack of sleep affects every aspect of our job. This same affliction is also claiming the lives of countless first responders on shift, off shift and after retirement. Delta Force operator Pat McNamara once stated that the special forces are often referred to as "disposable heroes". I think that is how first responders have been viewed for a long time as well.

We need to address both the work week and recovery from the high-stress shifts our profession endures. I hope these thoughts will sow some seeds in this occupation I love so much. "It's how we've always done it" has never been an acceptable answer; neither has "You knew what you signed up for". Our forebears paved the way with bunker gear, SCBAs, air monitors and a multitude of other progressive innovations. We need to be the generation that carries on this tradition by improving the physical and mental health of our peers. The athletes and special forces tactical athletes we revere have shown that ample rest and recovery are imperative to both performance and longevity. It's time we put our egos aside and treated first responders accordingly.

I'm tired of hearing the "last call". I know it's going to keep happening, but we truly have the power to reduce the number of deaths caused by this calling we love. This choice is completely in our power, although, as with every other change, there will be resistance by the ignorant and uninspired. I hope that the young firefighters of the future will look back and thank us for having the courage to change the very thing that is killing us. Tears will be shed, bells will be rung and flags will be folded. How many, though, is entirely in our hands.

Epilogue

I'm sitting on the back porch of my home as I write this. It's early morning in July, 2020. Nature's dawn chorus fills the warm summer air. The last four months have shown both the best and worst of society. A new has virus is sweeping across the planet, snatching lives as it goes. Families pray from isolation as their loved ones fight the virus, intubated in a hospital ICU. Healthcare workers spend entire shifts in full personal protective equipment, faces marred with the marks of the masks' straps. Heartbreaking images fill television screens and social media walls. Elderly married couples are separated by glass, as one visits their stricken soulmate, tear-filled eyes peering through a care home window. Densely populated cities like New York and London have truly been hit hard by the impact of the virus. The population has leant heavily on our first responders, doctors and nurses.

Some media outlets have capitalised on the fear produced by the pandemic. A death toll "counter" sits on the screen, climbing ever higher during their twenty-four-hour coverage. Death prediction maps further fuel the fire of terror. Fictional death toll percentages emerge, touting double figures, without any knowledge of how many have been infected or have overcome the virus. Images of hospitals overflowing, hallways full of patients have circulated in the news. Not one mention has been made of the fact that this is how many inner city hospitals look nearly year round. I've lost count of how many times I've waited four-plus hours to offload a patient to a hallway bed in an understaffed emergency room.

And then there's the underlying causes…

Although studies from every corner of the globe have shown that there is a much greater risk of morbidity from underlying health conditions, this fact was initially kept out of all mainstream coverage. Two extremist groups formed, tearing apart friendships. One side prophesied that the virus was a weapon of bioterrorism or a government plot. The other aimed squarely at shaming and even reporting any individual who was not cowering in fear in their home. The middle ground of sensibility has been lost through the cancerous distraction of society's squeaky wheels. Political parties have used the deaths to strengthen their campaigns, hurling blame at the opposition, using the victims as pawns in their quest for power.

Hundreds of thousands of people have died from a host of diseases since this pandemic began. There are two possible outcomes. Firstly, we walk away with the impression that hand sanitiser, masks and isolation are how we protect lives. That if we just hide in our homes, the virus will somehow miss us like a game of microorganism hide and seek. We ignore the ripple effects isolation has had on millions of people globally. We ignore the fact that the incidence of suicide, overdose, sexual abuse and domestic violence has swelled as positive outlets and responses were locked away from the people. We ignore the financial impact on the small businesses that couldn't weather the financial storm and the employees left furloughed or unemployed.

The alternative, one that actually honours those who have

tragically died, is that we address the health of our nation. The human body has survived millennia, exposed to the elements, through feast and famine. Our innate immune system has overcome the waves of bacteria and viruses that have swept across the planet since the dawn of time. Our ancestors lived in comparative filth, had minimal hygiene practices and yet the earth's population continued to grow. Knowledge of healthy practices has been passed from generation to generation. Which plants to eat, how to hunt and which insects to avoid. Movement was previously essential to survival, whether as nomads to follow food and the seasons or simply to find places to hunt, fish and gather.

Our response to the latest pandemic has exposed the vulnerability of modern human beings in the developed world. What has not been widely reported is that some places, including some of the less-developed countries around the world, have seen almost no deaths from coronavirus. The Japanese island of Okinawa, known for the highest density of centenarians per capita, had only eleven reported deaths at the time of writing of this book. Despite having a large elderly population, their world-renowned good diet and lust for life have clearly had a hand in their resilience. The entire country of Sweden, criticised for its social distancing leniency, has lost less than a quarter of the number of victims in New York City alone.

We have been led down a path of disease management that has served only the people who get rich from the drugs they peddle. This has created a false sense of security that a pill is a fix-all for any ailment that may materialise. This concept is tantamount to a group of medieval soldiers standing in an open field trying to prevent an invasion. They fight valiantly, fingers raw from drawing their bows, but are ultimately overrun. Now let's look at it from the other perspective. The soldiers build a castle with huge blocks of stone. They dig a deep moat, surrounding the structure with sharpened spikes lurking just below the water's surface. Cauldrons of boiling oil sit on top of the fifty-foot walls, ready to be poured on any invader rash enough to cross the lethal moat. Now, they can shoot arrows through the slits in the castle walls, from high above. Same invaders, different outcome.

The human body is no different. When given the correct nutrition, movement and recovery, it is a miracle of resilience. The physicality allows us to chase our food, run from predators and, if needed, fight. Our immune system, when optimised, can identify a foreign invader, have a relatively acute response and eliminate it. Conversely, if the body is sick, the immune response may be exaggerated as is seen with autoimmune disease, unrelenting as with cancer or simply ineffective as with AIDS. Our focus must be to foster resilience through physical and mental health. In 2016, the WHO found that almost two billion of the world's adults were overweight. This pandemic of obesity has been ignored for decades as companies jostle for monopoly over our food supplies. Tobacco kills more than eight million people a year yet cigarettes are still available in every shop.

We have a mental health crisis that is behind an estimated 800,000 suicides a year. Alcoholism kills 3.3 million people annually, with 31 million people reported as having drug-use disorders. There is no doubt that mental and physical health are completely interrelated. As communities bond, children play together and local sports teams converge, the healing effect of belonging further amplifies wellness.

Dependence on fossil fuels, industrial farming and undisciplined materialism has polluted the only home we have. We send men and women to space, exploring new planets as if ultimately planning to discard earth as we would a fast-food wrapper. During this period of global quarantine, Mother Nature has shown how quickly we can reverse the damage if we give her the chance. The canals in Venice are clearer, Indian mountains once hidden by smog are now visible and we're told even the holes in the ozone layer are closing. The health impact of these environmental changes cannot be underestimated. Cleaner air, water and soil mean healthier food and more resilient people. By restoring the planet, we heal its inhabitants too.

When I lived in Los Angeles, I often found a sad irony in hearing people argue back and forth about global warming, when their own city was enveloped in smog. This was another good analogy for extremism creating apathy. Focus on the things you can see; the freeways disappearing into a yellow haze in Burbank, the visible carbon after blowing your nose in London. Fix pollution and you'll heal the ozone layer. Support local organic farming and you'll stop our water supplies being poisoned by pesticides. Buy locally and you'll support community farms and vastly reduce pollution from transportation. Remove the chemicals from our food and you'll address significant causes of cancer and allergies.

After burying so many of my friends, I decided to start a podcast to bring the greatest minds in physical and mental wellness to the first responders, military and civilians of the world. With over three hundred episodes, the guests on the Behind the Shield Podcast are both numerous and varied. The world's most elite coaches discuss fitness. Farmers lend their insight on local, sustainable nutrition. Navy SEALs, Rangers and PJs impart wisdom on tactical medicine, defensive tactics and resilience. Firefighters, soldiers, police officers and nurses tell their powerful stories of trauma, depression and suicide attempts. Psychologists and psychiatrists relay the many tools available for overcoming mental ill health. The list goes on. This is a free library for you. The information is there and all you have to do is press play.

Every single life matters. This principle should be a constant in the communities and political arenas of the world, not just when Mother Nature pushes back. We are born into this incredible existence as a blank canvas, with the potential to do amazing things. We can create an environment where little children can thrive. An environment where healthy eating isn't a struggle but an innate decision that requires no effort. A world where movement is a large part of everyday life, utilising the incredible gift of the human body. We have an opportunity to make health so central that we have ample resources to help the downtrodden, the fallen and the frail.

The rock band Linkin Park asked us who cares if one more light goes out. I do.

∞

Acknowledgements

MY FIRST THANK YOU goes to my beautiful wife, Becky, and my boys, Tai and Ethan. You have shown the greatest of patience as a first responder family and I love you for it. Thank you for your sacrifice to our community.

To my mum, dad, brothers, sisters and grandparents, thank you for surrounding me with the core beliefs of kindness, compassion and gratitude.

Thank you to my good friend Josh Brolin for being my creative guiding hand during this process. Your mentorship teased this book out of my monkey mind.

I would also like to thank every single guest on the Behind the Shield Podcast. You have educated and enlightened me, volunteering your powerful stories or life's work to make a positive impact on this world. Without you, the podcast is nothing.

The Behind the Shield podcast aims to bring the greatest minds in physical and mental wellness to the first responders, military and civilians of the world. The guest list is deliberately diverse to help us step bravely out of the boxes we find ourselves in.

There are incredible survivor stories, from reformed Sierra Leone child soldiers to wounded Royal Marines. Experts in fitness, nutrition, sleep medicine, hydration and mobility discuss their philosophies on wellness. Some of the world's greatest sporting and tactical athletes detail their journey to physical and psychological excellence.

Mental health is a recurring theme. Psychologists and psychiatrists bring their medical expertise to the conversations. Men and women who have overcome anxiety, depression and even suicide attempts talk about their harrowing but important stories.

Most importantly, the podcast is free. A library of resources available to every single person on planet earth. All you have to do is press play.

Find the podcast at **www.jamesgeering.com** or on all podcast apps.

Made in the USA
Monee, IL
15 March 2024

6605cc34-3820-471c-a318-c8dee517c98cR01